SERMONS

ON SUBJECTS CONNECTED WITH

THE OLD TESTAMENT

SERMONS

ON SUBJECTS CONNECTED WITH

THE OLD TESTAMENT

BY
S. R. DRIVER, D.D.

REGIUS PROFESSOR OF HEBREW, AND CANON OF CHRISTCHURCH, OXFORD
EXAMINING CHAPLAIN TO THE LORD BISHOP OF SOUTHWELL

PUBLISHERS
Eugene, Oregon

Wipf and Stock Publishers
199 W 8th Ave, Suite 3
Eugene, OR 97401

Sermons on Subjects Connected with the Old Testament
By Driver, S.R.
ISBN: 1-59752-176-0
Publication date 5/6/2005
Previously published by Charles Scribner's Sons, 1892

PREFACE.

OF the Sermons collected in the present volume, the first five and the seventh were preached before the University of Oxford, the sixth was preached before the University of Cambridge, the last five were preached in the Cathedral at Christchurch.[1] The volume (the idea of which is due to the suggestion of a friend) may be regarded as supplementary, to a certain extent, to my *Introduction to the Literature of the Old Testament*, published in 1891. Although, as I hope, that work contained sufficiently clear indications that I was not indifferent to the theological aspect of the Old Testament, or to the permanent value attaching to the moral and religious teaching conveyed in it, the plan prescribed to me precluded my touching upon these subjects otherwise than incidentally; and the present volume, though not, of course, a systematic treatise, will, I trust, illustrate more completely how I view them, and in what directions I conceive that the Old Testament may be fruitfully and intelligently studied, and be made practically useful at the present day. It appears to be sometimes supposed that a critical view of the literature and history of the Old Testament is incompatible with any real sense for the spiritual and moral teaching which it contains : it is my hope and wish that the pages which follow may suffice to show how very far

[1] The first seven Sermons have been printed before, at the time when they were delivered, in the *Oxford University Herald*, the *Oxford Review*, the *Oxford Magazine*, or (No. 6) the *Cambridge Review*, Nos. 1 and 5 also in the *Church of England Pulpit and Ecclesiastical Review*.

this is from being the case. As I have said elsewhere, the adoption of critical conclusions, such as those which I have expressed myself, "implies no change in respect to the Divine attributes revealed in the Old Testament; no change in the lessons of human duty to be derived from it; no change as to the general position (apart from the interpretation of particular passages) that the Old Testament points forward prophetically to Christ."[1] The present collection of Sermons will, I hope, serve to illustrate, from different points of view, the truth of the positions here affirmed. It only remains to add that the last five sermons are of simpler structure than the rest, and are, in the main, more directly exegetical: my aim in publishing them has been to show more particularly how "the specific lessons of the Old Testament" may be enforced, and its "providential purpose" recognized,[2] without interpreting its words in a sense alien to their original meaning or context, or otherwise deviating from a strict application of critical and exegetical canons.

As an introduction, I have prefixed a Paper, read at the Church Congress at Folkestone, October 6, 1892, on the permanent moral and devotional value of the Old Testament for the Christian Church.

[1] *Introduction to the Literature of the Old Testament*, p. xv (ed. 4, p. xvi).
[2] Comp. Prof. A. F. Kirkpatrick's *Divine Library of the Old Testament* (1891), p. 118.

ADDENDUM.

Page 27, *note*.—The series of papers by Professor Ryle, here referred to, have been re-published in a single volume, under the title, *The Early Narratives of Genesis* (1892).

CONTENTS.

		PAGE
	ON THE PERMANENT MORAL AND DEVOTIONAL VALUE OF THE OLD TESTAMENT FOR THE CHRISTIAN CHURCH	ix
SERMON		
I.	EVOLUTION COMPATIBLE WITH FAITH	1
II.	ISAIAH'S VISION	28
III.	THE IDEALS OF THE PROPHETS	50
IV.	GROWTH OF BELIEF IN A FUTURE STATE ...	72
V.	THE HEBREW PROPHETS	99
VI.	THE VOICE OF GOD IN THE OLD TESTAMENT ...	119
VII.	INSPIRATION	143
VIII.	THE FIRST CHAPTER OF GENESIS	163
IX.	THE WARRIOR FROM EDOM	179
X.	THE SIXTY-EIGHTH PSALM	190
XI.	THE LORD OUR RIGHTEOUSNESS	204
XII.	MERCY, AND NOT SACRIFICE	217

THE PERMANENT MORAL AND DEVOTIONAL VALUE OF THE OLD TESTAMENT FOR THE CHRISTIAN CHURCH.[1]

THE subject on which I have been invited to read is one, I need hardly say, which it is impossible to treat with any approach to completeness in the limited space of twenty minutes. All that I can do is to illustrate briefly some of its more salient aspects, conscious all the time that I am leaving much unsaid, and fortunate in the thought that those who follow me will have the opportunity of supplying my omissions. Without in any degree derogating from the absolute ideal of life and conduct presented in the New Testament, I shall endeavour to show, in the time at my disposal, that the Old Testament possesses distinctive characteristics of its own, which must ever secure for it a paramount position and influence in the Church.

In the first place, then, and generally, the Old Testament has a value, peculiar to itself, from the fact that the truths which it inculcates are set forth with great variety of external form, and with superlative grace of imagery and diction. These features, though it is true they are but external ones, must not be under-rated in our estimate of the Old Testament as a whole. The preacher, not less than the poet or the orator, makes it his aim to impress,

[1] A paper read at the Church Congress at Folkestone, October 6, 1892.

by a choice and appropriate literary style, those whom he addresses; and had the truths which the Bible enunciates been presented in an unformed, uncultured literary garb, without the melody of rhythm and diction which actually accompanies them, we may be sure that its influence upon mankind would have been very much less than it has been. The variety of form, and the literary excellence, displayed in the Old Testament are both surprising. There is history, and biography, both penetrated, more or less visibly, by ethical and religious ideas; there is the oratory of Deuteronomy and the prophets, the aim of which is to enforce more directly the same truths; there is poetry, of varied types, lyrical, elegiac, and even—in a rudimentary form—dramatic, in which the emotions, fired by religious ardour, or suffused (Song of Songs) by a warm moral glow, find deep and pure expression. And each of these literary forms possesses, all but uniformly, that peculiar charm and grace of style, which entitles it to be ranked as "classical." History, oratory, poetry, each is of a type which, in its kind, cannot be surpassed: the bright and picturesque narrative of the historical books, the grand and impressive oratory of the prophets, the delicacy and brightness of the Hebrew lyric, vie alternately with one another in fascinating the reader, and compelling his admiration and regard.

But it is time to turn from the form of the literature of the Old Testament to its substance. And here it must at the outset be observed, that the provinces of morality and religion are in the Old Testament so closely associated that it is difficult to separate absolutely its moral and devotional aspects, and to treat them independently; moral duties are, for instance, often inculcated or exemplified in a manner which directly stimulates the devotional impulses; but as far as possible, I will deal with the two aspects of my subject successively.

(i.) 1. The Old Testament is of permanent value on account of the clearness and emphasis with which it insists on the primary moral duties, obligatory upon man as man; and not only on what may be termed the more private or individual virtues, but also on the great domestic and civic virtues, upon which the happiness of the family, and the welfare of the community, alike depend. Truthfulness, honesty, sincerity, justice, humanity, philanthropy, generosity, disinterestedness, neighbourly regard, sympathy with the unfortunate or the oppressed, the refusal to injure another by word or deed, cleanness of hands, purity of thought and action, elevation of motive, singleness of purpose—these, and such as these, are the virtues which, as we know, have ever evoked the moral admiration of mankind, and they are the virtues which, again and again, in eloquent and burning words, are commended and inculcated in the pages of the Old Testament. And corresponding to this high appreciation of moral qualities, there is its correlative—a hatred of wrong-doing, and a profound sense of sin, which is stamped, if possible, yet more conspicuously upon the literature of ancient Israel. I wish I had time to quote illustrations; but after all they would be superfluous; for those who hear me will, I am sure, be conscious already of familiar echoes sounding in their ears and substantiating what I have said. I will only observe, that such teaching is to be found in all parts of the Old Testament. Indirectly, for example, the moral value of qualities such as I have named is frequently illustrated in the historical books. The prophets devote their finest and most impressive periods to asserting the claims of the moral law upon the obedience of mankind, and to the rebuke of vice and sin. In the poetical writings, the Book of Proverbs abounds in similar moral teaching; while in the fifteenth chapter of the Book of Job, for instance, the agonies of a burdened conscience, and in the thirty-first chapter of the same book the portrait of a noble and elevated character, untainted even in secret by unworthy thoughts or evil desires, are drawn with surprising clearness and force of moral insight. Not only, however, are moral duties inculcated as such; the intimate connection of religion with morality is also strongly emphasized. The essential association of the religious character with the moral law is never lost from sight; and the moral conditions of pleasing God are repeatedly and unambiguously insisted on. Although the particular form in which this truth was commonly forgotten in ancient times, viz., the idea that God's favour could be propitiated by abundant sacrifices, irrespectively of the spiritual temper and moral dispositions of the worshipper, is no longer prevalent, yet there is still danger of its being overlooked in other ways. But in the Old Testament its importance is fully recognized; and the prophets, in passages glowing with warm and impassioned eloquence, set it forth with peculiar directness and force.

2. The Old Testament affords examples of faith and conduct, of character and principle, in many varied circumstances of life, which we may in different ways adopt as our models, and strive to emulate. It is not of course pretended that the characters of the Old Testament are devoid of flaws or blameless: some are limited by the moral and spiritual conditions of the age in which they lived, others exhibit personal shortcomings peculiar to themselves: but these faults are generally discoverable as such by the light of the principles laid down in the Old Testament itself, and none ought to be mistaken for virtues by members of the Christian Church, who alone on the present occasion come into consideration. In the historical books such virtues as kindness and fidelity, modesty and simplicity, courtliness of action and demeanour (implying self-discipline and repres-

VALUE OF THE OLD TESTAMENT. xiii

sion), patriotic feeling, domestic affection and friendship, are abundantly exemplified. In the narratives of events belonging to a distant past, from which precise historical reminiscences cannot reasonably be supposed to have been preserved, and in which therefore an ideal element may naturally be inferred to be present, the characters are so delineated as to be typically significant : the outlines supplied by tradition are so filled in by the inspired narrators with a living vesture of circumstance, expression, and character, that the heroic figures of antiquity become patterns to succeeding generations. The nobility, the dignity, the disinterestedness, the affection and love for his people, which mark the character of Moses, cannot but impress every reader. In the books of Samuel, in spite of faults, sometimes grave ones, we can trace, in the character of David, the softening and elevating influence of his religion; we can see that, both in his private and in his public capacity, he stood on a very different level from the heathen monarchs of antiquity. In a book like Ruth we can observe the religious spirit sanctifying and ennobling the ordinary duties of life : the fact that the scenes and conversations are doubtless to some extent idealized, and owe their form to the literary skill of the writer, does not detract from their didactic value; the picture, even if in particular features it reproduces the narrator's ideal rather than the actual and literal facts, is not less significant, not less instructive, as an example of life and manners, to ourselves. In the biographies of the prophets we see exemplified, partly in such details of their lives as have come down to us, partly, and more fully, in their discourses, sincerity of purpose, uncompromising opposition to vice and sin, devotion to principle, sympathy with suffering, national feeling, and generally a high and disinterested standard of moral action, maintained under many different circumstances, and in many varied situations of both public and private life, with a consistency and unflinching devotion which must command the admiration, and arouse the emulation, of all time.

3. The Old Testament is of permanent value on account of the great ideals of human life and society which it holds up before the eyes of its readers. I allude in particular to those ideal pictures of a renovated human nature, and transformed social state, which the prophets loved to delineate—the pictures of human nature, freed from the imperfections and corruptions which actually beset it, inspired by an innate devotion to God and right, and ruled not by law as a command dictated from without, but by moral impulses springing up instinctively within the breast: the pictures of human society, no longer harassed by the strife of opposing interests and parties, or honey-combed by oppressions and abuses, but held together by the bonds of love and friendship, each eager to advance his neighbour's welfare, and the nations of the earth united in a federation of peace under the suzerainty of the God of Israel. These ideals have, alas! not yet been realized so completely as the prophets anticipated: the passions and wilfulness of human nature have proved in too many cases obstacles insuperable even by the influences of Christianity; but progress, we may trust, has been made; and meanwhile these ideals remain, the wonder and the delight of the ages, to kindle our aspirations, to brace our efforts, to point out to us the goal which human endeavour should exert itself to realize, and which human society may one day hope to attain.

4. The Old Testament must always share with the New Testament the position of forming a standard of pure and spiritual religion, in contradistinction to all formalism or abstract systems. The parts of the Old Testament which might lend themselves, and in the late period of Jewish

VALUE OF THE OLD TESTAMENT.   xv

history did lend themselves, to exaggeration or perversion, in the direction of outward ceremonialism, are just those which were abrogated by the coming of Christ; and for those who do not live under the Levitical dispensation, the danger from this source has consequently passed away. The more directly moral and spiritual parts of the Old Testament display still the freshness and the power which they possessed when they were first written. The pure moral perceptions of the prophets, the unadulterated spiritual intuitions of the psalmists, must ever form a standard of faith and action, recalling men, when in peril of being led astray to trust in the external rites of religion, or to forget the true nature of spiritual service, to a sense of the real demands which God makes of His worshippers, and of the character and conduct in which He truly delights.

(ii.) I turn to consider the value of the Old Testament for devotional purposes. And here our thoughts move naturally, in the first instance, towards the Book of Psalms, in which the ripest fruits of Israel's spiritual experience are gathered together, and the religious affections find their richest and completest expression. It is difficult, within the compass of a few words, to characterize the Psalter with any adequacy. In the Psalter the religious affections manifest themselves without restraint, and the soul is displayed in converse with God, disclosing to Him, in sweet and melodious accents, its manifold emotions, its hopes and its fears, its desires and its aspirations. In the Psalms we hear the voice of penitence and contrition, of resignation and trust, of confidence and faith, of yearning for God's presence and the spiritual privilege of communion with Him, of reverential joy and jubilation, of thanksgiving and exultation, of confession and supplication, of adoration and praise; we hear meditations on the great attributes of the Creator, on His hand as seen in nature or in history, on the problems of human life, and on the pathos of human existence; and we hear all these varied notes uttered with a depth, an intensity, and a purity, which stand unparalleled in religious literature, and which the poets and hymn-writers of subsequent ages have been content to look up to as to an unapproachable model. Love, and trust, and faith, and such-like sacred affections, are set before us in the Book of Psalms, not as commanded, or enjoined as a duty from without, but as exercised, as the practical response offered by the believing soul to the claims laid upon it by its Maker, as the spontaneous outcome of the heart stirred by god-like emotions. The historical critic may question, and question justly, whether the Psalms are so largely as is commonly supposed a product of the earlier period of Israel's history: he will not question the justice of Dean Church's judgment when, in His well-known essay on the Psalms,[1] he claims that they lift us into an atmosphere of religious thought and feeling, which is the highest that man has ever reached, and that for their faith in the unseen, their perception of the character of God, and the manifold forms in which their affections expand and unfold themselves towards Him, their authors stand above the religious poets of every other age or clime, and enjoy a pre-eminence from which they can never be dethroned. As a devotional manual, as a manual displaying the soul in closest and yet freest and most manifold converse with God, the Book of Psalms must retain permanently in the Church the unique, unapproachable position which it has ever held.

Although, however, the devotional spirit finds its highest as well as its most familiar expression in the Psalter, it is by no means confined to this part of the Old Testament. As I remarked before, there are many parts of the Old Testament—for instance, the descriptions by the prophets of the

---

[1] In *The Gifts of Civilisation* (1880), p. 391 ff.

VALUE OF THE OLD TESTAMENT. xvii

marvellous attributes of the Deity, His glory, and majesty, and mighty acts—which, though not directly designed for devotional purposes, nevertheless arouse the emotions of adoration and wonder, and stir the devotional instincts. Thus the Book of Job, especially if read with the aid of a sympathetic commentary, such as that of Prof. A. B. Davidson (in the *Cambridge Bible for Schools*), will be found to contain, side by side with outbursts of defiant boldness, passages of supreme poetic delicacy, and instinct with devotional feeling, the sense of God's omnipresence and vastness, the moral significance of suffering, the pathetic yearning of the patriarch's soul to hear the voice of the Creator calling him again to His fellowship after the long period of seeming estrangement. The exilic chapters of the Book of Isaiah also contain frequent passages of the highest devotional suggestiveness and beauty: I may instance, in particular, the beautiful thanksgiving, confession, and supplication, contained in Is. lxiii. 7—lxiv. 12. There are besides numerous ideas, corresponding to different aspects of the devotional temper, which are presented with unique clearness and emphasis in the Old Testament. Consider, for instance, the warmth with which, in Deuteronomy, the love of God is insisted on as the primary motive of human action ;[1] how in the same book (nine times), and in writings influenced by it, the devotion of the whole being to God is expressed by the significant phrase, to search after, to serve, or to love Him, "with *all* the heart and with *all* the soul ; "[2] how, also in the same book, the injunction is reiterated, to "rejoice

---

[1] Deut. vi. 5, x. 12, xi. 1, 13, 22, xiii. 3, xix. 9, xxx. 6, 16, 20.
[2] Deut. iv. 29, vi. 5, x. 12, xi. 13, xiii. 3, xxvi. 16, xxx. 2, 6, 10 ; Josh. xxii. 5, xxiii. 14 ; 1 Kings ii. 4, viii. 48 ; 2 Kings xxiii. 3, 25 ; 2 Chron. xv. 12 (comp. the writer's *Introduction*, pp. 73, 94, 97, 190). The *heart* is mentioned as the organ, according to ancient Hebrew psychology, of the intellect (cf. Jer. v. 21 ; Hos. vii. 11, R. V. *marg.*), the *soul* as the organ of the desires and affections (cf. Deut. xii. 20, xiv. 26, xxiv. 15 [lit. "lifteth up his *soul* towards it"], Ps. xxv. 1, Is. xxvi. 9, Jer. xxii. 27, R. V. *marg.*, Mic. vii. 1).

before God" (viz. at a sacrificial meal) with a grateful and generous heart;[1] how in other books—for time compels me to speak generally—the fear of God, the observance of the ways, the commandments, the precepts of God, the resolution to obey Him and hearken to His voice, the desire to seek and to find Him, the determination to do His pleasure and to know Him, the privilege of the righteous to have access to God and to call upon Him at all times,[2] the blessedness of rejoicing, and even of delighting, in Him,[3] the joyousness of His service, the grateful sense of His protection or of His regard, are again and again expressed, and dwelt upon with an ardour which is never satisfied, with an enthusiasm which is unrestrained, with a devotion which knows no bounds. And it is, too, the high merit of the devotion of the Old Testament that it is always a manly devotion : in contrast to the tone of some modern writers, who have sought unwisely to surpass their models, the sentiment is never effeminate, the pathos never exaggerated or morbid. It is no small achievement, it may be observed in passing, to have framed what may almost be termed a complete devotional nomenclature, which formulates tersely and forcibly the great duties and offices of a spiritual religion, and which, moreover, with surprising elasticity, lends itself readily to adoption by another language. This, however, is what the religious teachers of ancient Israel have achieved. The illustrations which I have taken are but a few of the many devotional ideas with which the pages of the Old Testament abound, and which from the freshness, the force, and the reality, with which they are there set forth, must ensure for it undying vitality, and ever prevent it from becoming obsolete, or devoid of worth.

[1] Deut. xii. 12, 18, xvi. 11, xxvii. 7 (cf. xii. 7, xiv. 26, xvi. 14, xxvi. 11) : comp. Lev. xxiii. 40.
[2] Job xiii. 16, xxvii. 10, Ps. v. 7 ("can" or "do": not "will").
[3] Is. lxii. 10, &c. ; Is. lviii. 14, Job xxii. 26, xxvii. 10, Ps. xxxvii. 4.

I hold, then, that the moral and devotional value of the Old Testament—as indeed its religious value generally—is unaffected by critical questions respecting the authorship or date of its various parts. And if, in conclusion, I were to sum up briefly the grounds on which the moral and devotional value of the Old Testament seems to me to be permanently assured, I should say that these were partly its fine literary form, partly the great variety of mode and occasion by which the creed and practice of its best men are exemplified, partly the intensity of spirit by which its teaching is penetrated and sustained. As a purely literary work, the Old Testament combines the rare merits of including passages of high moral and spiritual worth, at once attractive and intelligible to the simplest capacities, and of being written in a style which must ever command the respect and appreciation of the most cultured. Then, secondly, the truths which it contains are not presented in an abstract garb, as a collection of moral or religious maxims to be apprehended merely by the intellect; they are presented under every variety of circumstance and form, as part of the actual life, and practice, and belief, of men representing a nation through the entire course of its chequered history. And they are presented, lastly, with a spirituality of motive, an intensity of conviction, a warmth and inwardness of feeling, and a singleness of aim, which cannot but impress deeply every reader, and evoke corresponding impulses in his own breast. Upon these grounds, it seems to me that so long as human nature continues, endowed intellectually as it now is, the Old Testament must remain an ever-fresh fountain-head of living truth, able to invigorate and restore, to purify and refine, to ennoble and enrich, the moral and spiritual being of man.

SERMON I.[1]

EVOLUTION COMPATIBLE WITH FAITH.

Gen. ii. 7 : "And the LORD God formed man of the dust of the ground, and breathed into his nostrils the breath of life ; and man became a living soul."

THESE words are taken from the opening section of the second of the two main documents, which have been interwoven with rare skill in our present Pentateuch, and which can be traced side by side to the close of the Book of Joshua. Both in scope and style, the two narratives differ widely ; the one deals with the antiquities of the Jewish nation, the origin of its sacred law, and its ceremonial observances, the other consists of a series of cameos of the patriarchal and Mosaic age, each exhibiting with singular perfection of literary form some theological or ethical truth. The portion which extends from the fourth verse of the second chapter to the close of the third chapter, is plainly a continuous whole, which appropriately follows the preceding section, because while that deals with creation as a whole, this places in the forefront the formation of man, and by detailing the story of

[1] Preached at St. Mary's, Oxford, before the University, on Sunday, Oct. 21, 1883.

the Fall forms the introduction to the subsequent history. The narrative, while not discrepant theologically from chapter i., is independent of it, and presupposes (as it would seem) a different view of the order of creation. Consider its opening words:—"No plant in the field was yet in the earth, and no herb of the field had yet sprung up;" (and the reason follows) "for Jehovah God had not caused it to rain upon the earth, and there was no man to till the ground." The surface of the earth is represented as desolate and bare: it is watered only by a mist. Upon the earth, thus bare, man is placed; a garden is prepared for his reception, and provided with trees necessary for his support. As yet he is alone in the world; and if the Hebrew of verse 19 is to be understood in its ordinary and natural sense, it implies that the animals were still non-existent—"And Jehovah God *proceeded to form*[1] out of the ground every beast of the field, and every fowl of the heaven; and brought them unto the man to see what he would call them." They pass before him in order, but amongst them all there is found no help "meet for him"—*i. e.* no help, corresponding, or adapted to him—in a single word, no consort. Only an origin most closely associated with himself can provide man with the social and intellectual complement which his nature lacks: he recognizes woman's equality with himself, and the work of creation is complete. The third chapter de-

---

[1] Such is the force of the Hebrew tense employed. Comp. the writer's *Hebrew Tenses*, § 76 *Obs.* (ed. 3, 1892, p. 88).

scribes how man's happiness was lost, and the contest with evil was begun, while intimating for him, in dark and enigmatic terms, the prospect of victory in the end.

How is this striking and impressive narrative to be viewed? Have we before us history, or what, for want of a better word, may be described as symbol or allegory? Have we before us a record of incidents occurring literally as they are related, or the embodiment, in a concrete, material dress, of theological verities, whose truth is to be sought in their substance, not in the form in which they are invested? There are more reasons than one which force this question upon us. Firstly, as we have seen, the narrative in the second chapter appears to be, not merely an expansion, or development, of that in the first chapter, but to deviate from it in detail. And secondly, the Hebrew records, when studied by the side of those belonging to other ancient nations, are seen to exhibit features which the current interpretation seems not sufficiently to explain; while recent years have shown that the Hebrew people were accessible to influences formerly unsuspected. It is now known, for instance, how wide was the diffusion of influences having their home in Babylonia; and there are features in these chapters of Genesis which (though, doubtless, not adequate to a demonstration) awaken in many minds a strong impression that some of their details are derived from that quarter. Is the admission of such a fact consistent with a belief in their inspiration? Or, should it prove to be well-founded, does it deprive the narrative of all value and authority? Many expositors have viewed the third chapter as allegorical; and when we consider the close connection subsisting between that chapter and the second, and the strong anthropomorphic colouring which pervades them both, it is not, it may be pleaded, unreasonable to interpret the former chapter as well upon the same principle. We can, at least, no longer shrink from estimating it afresh in the new light now thrown upon it; and if we have the interests of theology at heart, it will be our endeavour to show that a modified view of it is not irreconcilable with the just claims of our faith.

Is a literal history, then, the only form of narrative consonant with truth? Probably only custom has induced the common supposition that it is. And yet the Bible, it is obvious, avails itself, with the utmost freedom, of varieties of literary form. Poetry and parable, oratory and allegory, argument and feeling, appear there, as they appear in the literature of other civilized nations; the difference is that they are made, in a singular degree, the expression of the religious spirit, and the vehicle of religious truth. Human genius, not suppressed but quickened, not diverted from its natural lines of development, but directed in them, appears everywhere as the organ of the Divine Spirit. Should we not, then, by analogy expect to find the historians dealing similarly, not contenting themselves with a realistic treatment of history, but handling their subject, when its nature permitted it, with independence, and accommodating it to the purpose which they had in view? It is remarkable what a subordinate place the plain, unadorned chronicle holds in the Old Testament. If now it had been the object of the inspired writer to construct a picture of the beginnings of history, to which no traditions reached back, from which no records were handed down, and which is introduced, be it remembered, by no formula implying that it is an explicit revelation, what method can we suppose him to have followed, and what would be in harmony with his procedure elsewhere? The Biblical historians, it is plain, were dependent for their materials upon ordinary human sources; their inspiration shows itself in the application which they made of them, and the spirit with which they infused them. If the author of this part of Genesis had sought to give expression to certain truths respecting the nature of man and his relation to God, which he knew must have had an historical origin in the past, though the origin itself was concealed from him, what more appropriate method could he have adopted than that of throwing them into a quasi-historical form, selecting his materials from the sources available to him, and disposing them according to the principles which governed his entire work? If some of these materials were borrowed from an Assyrian or Babylonian source, others derived from the author's own reflection, only a limited and superficial view of the functions of the Biblical writers would conclude that the value or authority of his work was thereby impaired; its authority depends upon the place it occupies in the entire canon, its value upon the theological truths which it embodies, and which *ex hypothesi* are intact. And the test of the writer's inspiration is to be found in the depth and spirituality of his thoughts, and in the insight and discrimination with which, if such were actually his method, he wove his materials into a whole, adapted to take its place in the sacred canon. He did not, we may suppose, if this view be correct, receive a revelation respecting events long past; but a Divine intuition guided his thoughts, and enabled him to construct a picture, true ideally, and witnessing unmistakably to his inspiration, of the beginnings of man upon earth. But whatever its resemblance to Babylonian and other myths, be it greater or less than has been supposed, we may be sure that it concerns only the external dress. The more minutely Israelitish institutions and ideas are compared with those of their neighbours, the more conspicuous, among much that is similar, are the diversities, and the more plainly do we perceive that purer light which shone in their midst. This difference, fundamental though it is, does not exclude the use of forms of narrative analogous to, or even adapted from, those current in other countries; it only demands that, if adapted, they should be made subservient to truth, and be animated with the spirit of revelation.[1] And this, as we shall see, is here the case.

[1] Comp. Lenormant, *Les Origines de l'Histoire*, i., pp. xviii, xix, 106-7 (ed. 1880) : ii., pp. 263-269 (1882).

EVOLUTION COMPATIBLE WITH FAITH.

Let us, however, return to the text and inquire what it teaches us. Probably many readers suppose the significant term to be the expression *living soul*. This, however, is incorrect; for the Hebrew idiom uses *soul* more widely than we do, and applies it to any form of sentient life. In the first chapter, the same expression is used of the lowly organisms which move in the waters, and is rendered *living creature*.[1] In the verse before us, it means, then, that man became a living creature; implying, indeed, that he was possessed of his proper personality, but without defining its nature, or connoting any distinctive characteristic. Nor does the stress lie in the phrase, *breath of life;* this cannot differ essentially from the *spirit of life*, or the *breath of the spirit of life* which, in the seventh chapter,[2] appears as an attribute of animals in general. Does the author, then, recognize no pre-eminence appertaining to man? The subsequent narrative excludes such a supposition. No sooner does man find himself in presence of the other animals than his superiority is at once manifest; he evinces the faculty of reason; he gives names to them. Clearly the stress lies on the distinction drawn between man's corporeal frame, and those higher

[1] Gen. i. 20 (lit. "let the waters swarm with swarming things, even living souls"), 21 (lit. "all the living soul that creepeth, wherewith the waters swarm"). Similarly Lev. xi. 10, 46, Ezek. xlvii. 9; and of terrestrial animals, Gen. i. 24, 30 ("wherein there is a living soul"); ix. 10, 12, 15, 16. "Creature," where it occurs in these passages, is literally *soul*.
[2] Verses 15 and 22.

faculties imparted by a special act, symbolized in the word "breathed"—"breathed into his nostrils the breath of life." The animals are formed otherwise, in large and indiscriminate masses: man is formed as an individual, with direct personal relations with the Creator. The text declares that a spirit sent from God, and penetrating the material framework of the body, is both the source of life, and creates the human personality. The unique nature of man is its essential teaching.

But to this view, we hear it said, the facts are altogether fatal. Man did not come into being as a special creation, and has no such unique endowments as are here implied. He arose in accordance with well-defined laws of natural development out of anthropoid ancestors; and his pedigree is even carried further back, till its primitive source is discovered in a humble organism inhabiting the deep. Let us not recoil or lose our self-possession in face of such a contention. It is impossible for a man of average education to open a modern work on comparative biology without being aware of the flood of light which the conceptions of modern biologists have shed upon their science. Structures and organisms which seemed to be isolated, are shown unexpectedly to be connected with others, and in virtue of the connection are constituted parts of an intelligible whole. And though, from his imperfect acquaintance with the details, he may be unable to estimate the facts alleged at their true worth, he cannot fail to be impressed by the breadth and grandeur of the conception which gives a physical continuity to animate nature, and traces the innumerable living forms which teem upon the globe, to slow variation from a primitive stock. Gigantic as is the task imposed upon his imagination of realizing the course of development, it is lessened by the reflection that it has been spread over an inconceivable duration of time; and apart from difficulties that may present themselves from other quarters, the theory is so satisfying to his scientific instincts, so complete as a logical explanation of what appeared inexplicable, that he easily silences the objections which possibly occur to him. And those who have studied the subject intimately assure him, with daily growing confidence, that he need entertain no misgivings that the growth of species by a process of slow development (through the operation of causes which it is unnecessary now to dwell upon)[1] is an established fact. What position is the theologian here to assume? Is he to pass judgment upon the theory as *not proven?* Is he to point to the imperfections in the evidence, or to the assumptions which in his eyes appear unwarrantable? If he does so, he is in danger of not being listened to. In the first place, he is not conversant with the details; hence, the evidence upon which the theory is based does not come before him in its full cogency. The theory has, moreover, an intrinsic plausibility and

[1] But see J. B. Mozley, *Essays Historical and Theological,* ii., pp. 399-402.

reasonableness sufficient to compensate for some admitted deficiencies in its proof. And, secondly, he will lay himself open to the suspicion that he is opposing it at bottom, not upon logical or scientific grounds, but upon grounds of theology, and if this be the case, the contest upon which he enters is an uneven one; we may feel sure that, like questions of astronomy or geology in past days, the question of biology will be decided ultimately upon scientific grounds, and upon these alone.

Let me consider briefly the principal points at which theology and science come, or appear to come, into collision.

1. Science disputes with great earnestness and persistency the doctrine of special creations. She declares that the evidence in favour of development is incontrovertible, and that the facts of geology imply, on the assumption that species were created separately, an arbitrary method of procedure, devoid of principle or rule.[1] It must be conceded that the theory of special creations exempts the origin of species from the operation of natural law. It can cause no surprise that science opposes this limitation of her prerogative, and resents the prohibition of speculation upon matters which lie evidently within her legitimate domain. I cannot think that theology has here a right to interfere. The issue is not whether the growth of species by the operation of natural processes be accepted as a fact or not; not whether

[1] T. H. Huxley, *Lay Sermons*, pp. 280-3 (ed. 1874).

you or I are personally convinced of its truth; but whether, as theologians, we can demur to it. The two issues are sometimes confused; but it is of the first importance to keep them distinct. The theory, thus far, affirms nothing as to the origin of life, or as to the power by which its development may be guided; it affirms merely that it has developed according to physical laws, of the working and nature of which it declares itself to be cognizant. There is nothing here for theology to shrink from. Or is such a theory to be met by an appeal to the first chapter of Genesis? It appears to be certain that the progression laid down in that chapter is at variance, in some particulars, not with the hypotheses of biologists, but with the facts of palæontology; and this circumstance is an indication that to use it for that purpose is to mistake its import, and to misunderstand its position in the Old Testament Canon. The object of that chapter is not to give an authoritative record of the history of the globe, but to show, by a series of representative pictures, that alike in its origin and in the stages through which it has passed it has been dependent upon the presence, and has given effect to the purposes, of Almighty God.[1] Science, as such, cannot deny this; she only says, and says quite truly, that it is a question with which she is not concerned. But the theologian, instead of cavilling at the theory, ought rather to be grateful to science for having enabled him to fill in the outline

[1] See more fully below, Sermon vii.

sketched in Genesis with such glorious colours, and for having opened his mind to comprehend the magnificent scheme of continuity which dominates nature, which binds together with this earth the remotest heavens, and which it has been the labour of untold ages even partially to unfold. Or has he forgotten the memorable words by which, with almost prophetic intuition, his own revered teacher solved in anticipation the difficulty which future years would bring: "Men are impatient and for precipitating things, but the Author of nature appears deliberate throughout His operations, accomplishing His natural ends by slow successive steps"?[1]

2. Let me pass to a second question. The quarrel with final causes is an old one; and the sound of strife has not ceased yet. Doubtless, Bacon was right; doubtless, the final cause has been prematurely and superficially resorted to, to the injury of true science; doubtless, there is ground for the bitterness of spirit with which, in the books of some modern physicists, the subject is alluded to. The explanation of an organ or structure as being designed to fulfil some function, is discarded; the organ has not been designed *in order* to perform its function; it owes its existence to the fact that it has performed its function, and performed it well, in the past; a useful variation has survived, and been improved; others, which proved themselves useless, perished. The explanation by mechanical or physical causes is,

[1] Butler, *Analogy*, Part II., chap. iv. (towards the end).

therefore, it is urged, sufficient. No room or need is left for the final cause. And some satisfaction is evinced in pointing to structures, which are not frequent in nature, useless, or worse than useless, to their possessors. The examples are grouped under a special rubric, bearing the significant name of *dysteleology*. But again, it must be clearly understood what the issue is. Theology is not concerned with the explanation of particular organs or structures: all that she desires to know is, whether their explanation *collectively*, whether the explanation of the totality of phenomena constituting the organic world, by means of physical or mechanical laws, is incompatible with the belief in a presiding purpose. Rudimentary organs, she declares, do not trouble her; she is aware that God works by general laws, which may be expected sometimes to result in such phenomena. She does not seek to discover directly the purpose of each structure, but she has a belief that nature, as a whole, is the embodiment of a purpose. Is she at liberty to retain this belief? She is willing to concede that the explanation of nature by mechanical principles (so far as it has been carried) does not *necessitate* that belief; but are these principles compatible with it? Do they exclude it? It is said, for instance,[1] that "just the most difficult problems, which once teleology alone seemed capable of solving, are those which have now been solved mechanically by the theory of descent. Everywhere

[1] Haeckel, *Evolution of Man*, i., p. 16.

we are enabled to substitute unconscious causes acting from necessity, for conscious causes, involving a purpose." The antithesis, thus crudely stated, is an unreal one; but let that pass. We may be enabled to make this substitution; the question which interests us is, Are we obliged? It nowhere appears that we are. Men of science are jealous of the introduction of the idea of the final cause at particular points in the organic series. They think, and justly, that to admit it is to abnegate one of their most valued rights; but to those who, for reasons not within the cognizance of science, choose to view the entire series as the manifestation of a purpose, they have nothing to oppose.[1] As before, they may personally disbelieve it, but all that they can logically object is, that the subject lies beyond their province, and that, as students of science, they profess no opinion upon it. It is the vainest and shallowest of illusions to imagine that by discovering causality, we are disowning purpose, or displacing mind. We are but disclosing the methods through which mind works, and purpose is displayed.[2] There is, of course, a larger question, whether, namely, the mechanical explanation of the facts of organic nature has left intact the proof, drawn therefrom, of the existence of a Designer; but with this question, though much might be said upon it, I am not concerned to-day.

[1] Huxley, *Critiques and Addresses* (1883), p. 307.
[2] See J. Martineau, "Modern Materialism, its Attitude towards Theology," in the *Contemporary Review*, xxvii., p. 542, reprinted in *Essays, Reviews, and Addresses* (1891), vol. iv. p. 257.

Here also, then, if we rightly define the lines of demarcation, there is no real antagonism between theology and science : on the contrary, the discovery of the physical cause is essential, unless our idea of the final cause is to be an empty one, and its use a cloak for ignorance.

3. The issue becomes a graver one when the theory is applied to man. Nevertheless, it is argued, the facts are so strong, that it is impossible to exclude him from its operation : he is but the last and highest stage in the long evolutionary series ;[1] nor, it is added, do his intellectual faculties differ, except in degree, from those of the brute creation.[2] The latter assertion need not now detain us : the premises upon which it depends are not, properly speaking, data of science ; and philosophy unconditionally refuses its assent.[3] The first assertion, understood strictly, affirms no more than that man's bodily frame has been developed in the manner described ; only in his bodily frame are the analogies detected which decisively connect him with other creatures, and only this is the subject of scientific observation. Individual men of science sometimes deny to him the existence

[1] Huxley, *Man's Place in Nature*, p. 108 ; Haeckel, *History of Creation*, ii., p. 360 f.

[2] *Lay Sermons*, p. 339 ; Haeckel, *Generale Morphologie*, ii., p. 430 f.

[3] *Edinburgh Review*, April 1883, pp. 452-7—a masterly criticism, in an essay entitled "Modern Ethics," since owned by W. L. Courtney, and reprinted by him in *Constructive Ethics* (1886) ; see pp. 270-277.

of a soul; but, when pressed, they commonly allow their meaning to be that they can find no evidence of a soul, that their methods of inquiry do not lead them to it; that its existence is no scientific postulate.[1] This, however, is something very different from the assertion that science leaves no room for it, and is, indeed, so obvious as to be scarcely better than a truism.

Does it seem possible that we can, as theologians, accept this theory of the origin of our race? There might be no conclusive objection against accepting it as an explanation of man's bodily frame;[2] but can we separate the material organism from the immaterial soul? Or will the reality and independence of the latter, which is affirmed (it is important to remember) not by theology only, but by the impartial judgment of philosophy, be prejudiced by the admission? We should be better able to answer these questions, were we more fully acquainted than we are with the nature of the immaterial principle in man, of that which we recognize in ourselves as the seat of consciousness, as the feeling and thinking self. Alas! we can discover and analyse the laws by which its acts and functions are regulated; we can trace, in a thousand instances, its wonderful correlation with the structure of the brain; but of its origin or nature we

---

[1] Comp. Bishop Cotterill, *Does Science aid Faith?* (1883), pp. 158, 195 bottom, 199.
[2] Comp. the citation in Drummond, *Natural Law in the Spiritual World*, p. 225.

EVOLUTION COMPATIBLE WITH FAITH.

can add nothing to what the text declares, "And Jehovah God breathed into his nostrils the breath of life, and man became a living soul." The question which was asked by Lucretius, *Nata sit an contra nascentibus insinuetur*, was left unanswered by Augustine; and remains unanswered still. We can only say that it has pleased Almighty God by some law, hitherto undiscovered and perhaps undiscoverable, to unite, under certain conditions, a material organism with an immaterial soul. We are in presence of a mystery which defies explanation at the hand of man, which says, " Thus far shalt thou come, and no further." We arrive at something super-sensual, at something which imagination cannot figure, nor reason comprehend, something which asserts its presence while it eludes our grasp, and which, if we seek relief from our perplexity by denying its existence, rises up against us and overwhelms us with confusion of face. Nevertheless, a recognition of this fact in the individual may not be without its service when we pass to the wider problem presented by the race. Let it be admitted that physical causes explain in the individual the growth of his bodily frame; they throw no light on the origin of the soul. What if the case should be similar when the first man appeared upon this earth? What if, with the race then, as with the individual now, Almighty God ordained the completion of the bodily structure by the same laws which he has imposed upon all organic nature, until the unknown conditions were satisfied, in virtue of which the dawning intelligence was manifested in it? In this case what science postulates is granted. All that an observer, supposed to be present, would have traced, would be in accordance with those laws, whose uniform and unvarying operation science everywhere discerns. Only the super-sensual fact, over which she asserts no rights, would have been beyond his reach.

For, if we think to expel the super-sensual from nature, we embark upon a hopeless task. There are phenomena which *will* not be explained by the premises of materialism. There are facts which cannot by any intelligible process of thought be connected with the data of sense. There is, within each one of us, a permanent and undying witness to the reality of the super-sensual—the fact of consciousness. While human consciousness survives, philosophy has an unassailable basis on which to assert for mind, whencesoever derived, its independence and supremacy. Here is a fact which no theory of the origin of human consciousness can get rid of, and which any theory having a claim to validity must preserve intact.

Is such a view of the union of soul and body unscientific? Does it introduce a secret flaw into the symmetry of nature, and break down the hardly-won conception of her unity? It can do so in the eyes of those alone who, implicitly if not ostensibly, hold that the senses are the measure of reality. Strange illusion! We may ascertain the laws and conditions under which one body acts upon another; we may watch, under a microscope, the change and growth of a living organism; but how it is at all, that one material particle is influenced by another, or what the hidden agency is, which causes the organism to develop, is beyond our grasp.[1] The widest observation brings the mystery no nearer: we understand the surface better; we do not penetrate beneath it. The admission that this is the case is often made verbally;[2] but it carries with it some important consequences. It removes the antecedent objection that there is no mystery in nature, nothing inscrutable, nothing in the full sense of the word inexplicable. If there is one mystery, there may be more. If comprehension fails us in one direction, it may fail us in another. Now, science is satisfied, if we grant continuity in the development of living things; it admits that on the origin of life, it has no information to offer[3]—it only asks that, the germs being given, we should hand over their development to the operation of fixed laws. How these laws were fixed, whence matter acquired the properties with which, as we know it, it is invested, it does not presume to say; it leaves us free to make what assumptions we choose, provided we do not claim either to derive them from science, or to impose them upon it. Here then we leave science: it is admitted on both sides, that science, as such, teaches nothing respecting

[1] Lotze, *Mikrokosmus*, i., p. 310 f.
[2] Haeckel, *Generale Morphologie*, i., p. 105; Huxley, *Lay Sermons*, p. 341, *Critiques and Addresses*, p. 285.
[3] *Encyclopædia Britannica*, 9th ed., vol. viii. (1878), p. 746.

super-sensual entities, and as such, therefore, possesses no knowledge of God or of the soul. If we have knowledge of these realities, as we believe them to be, from other sources, we are at liberty to make use of it, provided we in no way infringe the continuity and fixity which science so jealously guards. As we are not dealing here with what in the technical sense of the term are described as " miracles," we shall not do so. We are at liberty, then, to believe, for example, what is taught by all deeper philosophy, that the world as known can only subsist in a mind that thinks it. Or, again, we are at liberty to hold the belief that the personal Creator of the world is also its ever-present Sustainer, and by means known to Him, but unimaginable by us, ordains those effects of which our senses discern but the outside form. This fact is one which of course no theist will dispute; I have not made use of it before, because it was not required by the argument. It lies, indeed, outside the scope of science, and we freely admit that it cannot be demonstrated by science. It is not, however, on this account in antagonism to it: for science only asks for fixed laws; and it has long been a commonplace of theology that fixed laws are the form through which, as a rule, the Creator has been pleased to carry out His purposes.

But if we realize the truth that Almighty God is *everywhere* present, everywhere manifesting His power, not merely on those occasions which we distinguish as miraculous, but in the normal and regular processes of nature, the gain is great and our view becomes at once clearer. The fear is seen more distinctly to be groundless, lest by conceding a scheme of evolution we are prejudicing the Divine supremacy. We are conceding merely a change in the mode by which it is manifested. As regards the question which here concerns us, we are not bound to maintain a particular theory. On the one hand, if it be true—to quote the words of one whom Oxford has not yet ceased to mourn—if it be true that "countless generations passed, during which a transmitted organism was progressively modified till an eternal consciousness could realize, or reproduce itself in it, then this might add to the wonder with which the consideration of what we do, and are, must always fill us, but it could not alter the results of that consideration."[1] It could not, that is, alter the view which we had reached, upon independent grounds, of the nature of human intelligence. If, by an act inscrutable to us, the foundations of human personality were laid in the remote past, it would but add one to the many mysteries by which our being is surrounded, it would but be a fresh illustration of the adorable wisdom of God. It is not demanded of us that we should abandon what is certain for the sake of assumed inferences from that which is uncertain. If, on the other hand, supposing the alternative to be a real one, we hold that intelligence supervenes in each

[1] T. H. Green, *Prolegomena to Ethics*, p. 87 f. Comp. Lotze, *u.s.*, i., p. 138 (3rd ed.).

individual case, as it were separately and from without, then a recognition of the same truth of God's continual presence may help us to understand how this is no arbitrary interference. It ceases to be an assumption void of presumption or analogy, that in the midst of the processes observable by the senses, He may manifest Himself in other ways not so observable, and only traceable inferentially. Mere visibility cannot surely, as appears sometimes to be tacitly assumed, constitute the criterion of God's operation. The operation of His power, we may rest assured, is not unregulated by law, though the law which regulates it may involve factors which our faculties are not adequate to discover. It is no longer, if the familiar illustration may be permitted, a *Deus ex machinâ* to which we have recourse; it is rather, to retain the metaphor, a *Deus in scenâ*, whose glory, filling heaven and earth, bursts upon our opened eyes. To be sure, such reasonings will be rejected as futile by materialism; but they come into no collision with science. Science does not frame a theory of the universe as a whole, it deals only with the laws which govern the material part of it: a theory of the whole must find room for other facts, other phenomena, other laws, not less than for those which form the subject-matter of science.

Let theology, then, offer no hindrance to at least a provisional acceptance of this theory of the origin of man. More than a provisional acceptance cannot, I venture to think, be at present demanded of those who are not experts. The admission, if made, will not, after what I have said, be misconstrued. We would gladly know more respecting the influences to which specifically man's origin is due, and of his condition, and thoughts, when he first awoke to self-consciousness. But science is here silent. What, then, is the relation of the two records with which the Bible opens, to this, or other physical theories? They are not a substitute for science; they do not speak where she is silent. They do not pretend to supersede science, or to impede a sympathetic interest in her progress, and a cordial acceptance of her discoveries. They guide us upon different principles. They afford us certain clues, which without their aid we might not have discovered, and assuredly should not have grasped so firmly. They recall to our mind truths to which science could never lead us. Their purport is theological, not historical; hence, they speak by pictures which are true substantially if not in detail, which appeal powerfully to the imagination, and impress themselves readily upon the memory. The first record teaches us that God is a Spiritual Being, prior to the world, and independent of it, that the world arrived at the form in which we know it by a series of stages, each the embodiment of a Divine purpose, and the whole the realization of a Divine plan; that man, in particular, among the other animals, is endowed with a distinctive pre-eminence, signified by the term "the image of God." These are *fundamental* thoughts, which science cannot

SERMON I.

dispute, and which experience testifies. How clearly and distinctly the narrator sets them before us! Let it not be forgotten that in the Babylonian cosmogony to which I alluded,[1] these truths are entirely lost sight of, gods and world being there evolved together, with naïve impartiality, out of the same abysmal chaos.[2] The second record teaches us the double nature of man—his earthly frame, and the spirit communicated to him from the Creator, enabling him to apprehend intellectual and religious truth. It seizes a fact, which may have taken actually long ages to accomplish, and represents it under a forcible, concrete image which all can understand. It tells us how the earth is fitted for his abode, and designed to supply him with maintenance. It tells us how he first used his reason by the creation of language, distinguishing objects from one another, and from himself. It tells us how, by some mysterious process, which even science can scarcely hope to define with precision, the bifurcation of the sexes was effected, and how the difference between them has a deep ethical and social significance. It tells us, by a dim allegory, which speaks, however, only too distinctly to every child of Adam, how man became conscious of a moral law, and how upon the first temptation he broke it. These are truths of man's natural life; it will be seen

---

[1] It may be read in Schrader's *Cuneiform Inscriptions of the Old Testament* (1883), on Gen. i. 1, 14, 20; or in *Records of the Past*, second series, i. (1888), p. 133 ff. (in a different version, p. 149 ff.).

[2] See the references given below in the course of Sermon vii.

at once that though the style of representation is different, they agree in conception with what we read in chapter i., and are indeed mostly involved in the gift or capacity there denoted by the "image of God." Here, then, is their inherent, inalienable value—a value which is unassailable by criticism, and which is superior to all questions of authorship or date. I do not, for example, seek to reconcile the first chapter of Genesis with palæontology or astronomy, for it seems to me that in some particulars they are not reconcilable: but this very fact teaches me a truer estimate of its import; and I claim it as the foundation of a religious contemplation of nature. Science warns us that we have been wrong in insisting upon a strictly literal interpretation; historical criticism comes forward and shows us how, without prejudice to theology, we may abandon it.[1] It shows us how what was once treated as historical, may be regarded as symbolical; and how, as thus understood, the theological teaching of Genesis accords with what a progressive revelation might be expected, from analogy, to contain.

A readjustment of the relations subsisting between theology on the one hand, and criticism and science on the other, is beginning to be recognized as one of the pressing needs of the time. A first step towards

---

[1] Comp. a Sermon by the Rev. C. Gore, Vice-Principal of the Theological College, Cuddesden (now Principal of the Pusey House, Oxford), printed in the *Oxford Magazine*, Nov. 28, 1883, p. 419.

this readjustment is a more precise definition of the border-line between them. And a second step is a just recognition of the limits at which knowledge fails us. Among the conclusions at which criticism and science claim to have arrived, are many which, when impartially examined, are found to have no relation with Christian truth, and which, therefore, the Christian believer is free to estimate upon their intrinsic merits. The antagonism lies not with the scientific fact, not even with the scientific theory, but with a philosophic creed, which forms no part of them, is in no way involved in them, and with which they are temporarily associated only through the prepossessions of particular advocates.[1] In the minds of many, by an unfortunate but intelligible confusion, the plausibility of the theory becomes evidence for the plausibility of the creed. Ought it not to be the aim of those who can see more distinctly to aid in removing this confusion, by owning the theory while discarding the creed? Christian thinkers, by too often holding aloof, lend support to the false identification of scientific speculation with pantheism or atheism, and place in their opponents' hands a weapon, the strength of which they seem singularly to ignore. But a movement, full of promise and hope, has shown itself recently in a different direction. May the Source and Author of Truth not abandon the creatures whom He has made; may He dispel from their eyes the mists of error, and bid the light shine within their

[1] Comp. Bishop Cotterill, *u.s.*, pp. 104, 212.

EVOLUTION COMPATIBLE WITH FAITH.

hearts, till they attain more perfectly the knowledge of His ways![1]

[1] See now, further, in support of the general line taken in the preceding Sermon, the able treatment of the same subject by the late Aubrey L. Moore in *Science and the Faith* (1889), pp. xi—xlvii, pp. 162-221 (a reprint of three articles on "Darwinism and the Christian Faith," published originally in the *Guardian*, Jan. and Feb. 1888), and pp. 222-235 ("Recent Advances in Natural Science in their relation to the Christian Faith," a paper read at the Reading Church Congress, Oct. 1883). See likewise A. M. Fairbairn, "Theism and Science," in *The City of God*, pp. 35-74 (ed. ii., 1886). And on the early narratives of Genesis comp. Prof. H. E. Ryle in the *Expository Times* (T. & T. Clark, Edinburgh), April, June, Sept., Dec., 1891, Feb. 1892.

SERMON II.[1]

ISAIAH'S VISION.

Isaiah vi. 3: "And one cried unto another, and said, Holy, Holy, Holy, is the LORD of Hosts: the whole earth is full of his glory."

THE chapter from which these words are taken forms the first lesson for this morning's service. It would be difficult to find a more appropriate chapter for the day on which we celebrate the highest mystery of the Christian faith than the one in which Isaiah, admitted in spirit behind the veil which severs the visible from the invisible world, describes in dignified and impressive language, the vision presented to his eyes. As in other cases, the framework of the vision is formed by the objects with which the prophet was familiar; and the vision is itself conditioned by his mental power and spiritual capacity. The grandeur and richness of Isaiah's imagination pre-eminently fits him to be the recipient of a vision which transcends those of Amos, Jeremiah, or Ezekiel, and indeed stands unique in the Old Testa-

---

[1] Preached in the Chapel of New College, Oxford, before the University, on Trinity Sunday, May 31, 1885.

ment. The scene, then, which Isaiah beholds, is the heavenly palace of Jehovah's sovereignty, modelled upon, but not a copy of, His earthly Temple at Jerusalem: "I saw the Lord sitting upon a throne, high and lifted up, and his train filled the temple." The comparatively small adyton of the Temple on Zion is indefinitely expanded, the lofty throne takes the place of the mercy-seat, the skirts of the royal mantle, falling in ample folds, fill the space about and below the throne, and conceal from the beholder, standing beneath, the unapproachable Form seated upon it. The two colossal cherubim, whose extended wings overshadowed the ark in the Holy of Holies, are absent, and there appears instead a choir of living creatures encircling the throne: "Seraphim stood above him: each one had six wings; with twain he covered his face, and with twain he covered his feet, and with twain he did fly." The seraphim are not mentioned elsewhere, and the origin and meaning of the name can only be supplied by conjecture. It must suffice to say that they appear here as the most exalted ministers of the Divine Being, in immediate proximity to Himself, and give expression to the adoration and reverence unceasingly due from the highest of created intelligences to the Creator. Possessed apparently of human form, and in an erect posture, they form a circle—or perhaps rather a double choir—about the throne, each with two of his wings seeming to support himself upon the air, with two covering his face, in reverence, that he might not gaze directly upon the Divine glory, and with two his own person, in humility, not deigning to meet directly the Divine glance. Can the scene be more aptly or more worthily reproduced than in our own poet's noble lines ?—

> "Fountain of light, thyself invisible,
> Amidst the glorious brightness where thou sitt'st,
> Throned inaccessible, but when thou shad'st
> The full blaze of thy beams, and through a cloud
> Drawn round about thee like a radiant shrine
> Dark with excessive bright thy skirts appear,
> Yet dazzle heaven, that brightest Seraphim
> Approach not, but with both wings veil their eyes."[1]

Isaiah, standing as it were by the doorway, hears the seraphs' hymn of adoration ; and as the sound of their united voices—such is the force of the expression in verse 4—reverberated through the vast expanse above, the pillars of the door shook to their foundation, and the space around was filled with smoke, symbolizing, as it would seem, the manifestation of God in act or word. Isaiah, overpowered for the time by the vision, as he recovers self-possession, is conscious only of his unworthiness to be where he is. Unlike the seraphs, he is a man of unclean lips: his connection with his nation cannot save him, for it is unclean likewise: "Woe is me," he exclaims, "I am undone." But an altar is there, with a fire burning upon it, the fire, apparently, which as it consumes the incense cast upon it, betokens the Divine acceptance ; and one of the seraphs, taking from it a burning coal,

[1] Milton, *Paradise Lost*, iii. 375 ff.

touches the prophet's lips with it, and pronounces him absolved. Only then is he reassured and ready, when he hears the invitation, " Who will go for us ? " with generous ardour, knowing not whither the call may carry him, regardless of the sacrifice which it may cost, to offer himself for the work. It may be regretted, upon general grounds, that the authors of our Lectionary, by omitting the three last verses in the narrative, have deprived the lesson of its true conclusion ; but the verse which I have selected will afford more than sufficient materials for our purpose to-day.

Two of the Divine attributes form the theme of the seraphs' hymn—God's holiness as inherent in Himself, His glory as manifested in the earth. Holiness, the first of these, denotes fundamentally a state of freedom from all imperfection, specially from all moral imperfection ; a state, moreover, realized with such intensity as to imply not only the absence of evil, but antagonism to it. It is more than goodness, more than purity, more than righteousness : it embraces all these in their ideal completeness, but it expresses besides the recoil from everything which is their opposite. This is the sense which the word bears throughout Scripture. Israel is to be a holy nation ; it is separated from the other nations of the earth, in order that it may reflect in idea the same ethical exclusiveness which is inherent in its God.[1] The " Holy One of Israel," that fine designation, which is first used by Isaiah, and was probably indeed

[1] Ex. xix. 6, Lev. xx. 26, Deut. vii. 6, xxvi. 19.

framed by him as the permanent embodiment of the truth so vividly impressed upon him in this vision, is a title which would remind the Israelite as he heard it of this distinctive attribute of his God, and arouse him to the duty of aiming after holiness himself. Holiness, again, is the attribute which in virtue of the tie uniting Jehovah and His people, prophets saw vindicated in their deliverance from tyranny or oppression: "The LORD hath made bare his holy arm in the eyes of all the nations"[1]; or "And the heathen shall know that I am the LORD, when I shall show myself holy[2] in you before their eyes." And so it is to God's holiness that the Psalmist, persecuted but conscious of innocence, who has cried day and night without respite, appeals: "And thou art holy, who inhabitest the praises of Israel."[4] Passages from the New Testament I need not here quote. The seraphs celebrate God not as the All-righteous, not as the All-powerful, or the All-wise; they celebrate Him under a title which expresses His essence more profoundly than any of these, and which marks more significantly the gulf which severs Him from all finite beings: they celebrate Him as the All-holy.

But not only does the seraphic hymn celebrate the Divine nature in its own transcendent purity and

[1] Isa. lii. 10.
[2] Or, "get me holiness" (cf. "get me glory," Ex. xiv. 4, where the conjugation in the Hebrew is the same), *i. e.* get myself recognized as holy. Comp. A. B. Davidson's *Ezekiel* in the *Cambridge Bible for Schools*, pp. xxxix, xl, 279.
[3] Ezek. xxxvi. 23.   [4] Ps. xxii. 3.

ISAIAH'S VISION.

perfection: it celebrates it as it is manifested in the material world—" The fulness of the whole earth is his glory." By "glory" we mean the outward show or state attendant upon dignity or rank: the glory, then, of which Isaiah speaks, is the outward expression of the Divine nature: pictured as visible splendour it may impress the eye of flesh; but any other worthy manifestation of the Being of God may be not less truly termed His glory. It is more than the particular attribute of power or wisdom; it is the entire fulness of the Godhead, visible to the eye of faith, if not to the eye of sense, in the concrete works of nature, arresting the spectator and claiming from him the tribute of praise and homage. It is that which in giant strokes is imprinted upon the mechanism of the heavens, and which, in the bold conception of the poet, " One day telleth another, and one night declareth to another," so far as the empire of heaven extends.[1] It is that which, as another poet writes, in the thunderstorm, when the clouds seem to part and disclose the dazzling brightness within, wrings from the denizens of God's heavenly palace the cry of adoring wonder.[2] Conceived, again, as an ideal form of splendour, it is set by Isaiah before the Israelites as that which should be the object of their reverence, but which has been too often the object of their shamelessness and scorn—" For their tongue and their doings are against the LORD, to defy the eyes of his glory." [3] It is the attribute which is disclosed when those who

[1] Ps. xix. 1, 4.   [2] Ps. xxix. 9.   [3] Isa. iii. 8.

are the enemies of truth and right are overcome, and the kingdom of God extended upon earth.[1] "Be thou exalted, O God, above the heavens: be thy glory over all the earth," prays the Psalmist:[2] let Thy majesty be acknowledged more widely, more worthily, than it now is, amongst the nations of the world. The movements of history, in so far as they affect the welfare of Israel and promote God's purposes of salvation, are a progressive revelation of His glory: "Every valley shall be exalted, and every mountain and hill shall be brought low," before the nation returning from its exile, "and the glory of the LORD shall be revealed, and all flesh shall see it together."[3]

The text, however, speaks without any limitation: "The fulness of the whole earth is his glory." Do the words relate to the present only, or do they embrace as well the ideal consummation which was then—as it is now—still future? We cannot say. We must be content to understand the meaning to be that the glory is objectively there already; though it is consonant with what other prophets express to suppose that, as history advanced, it would be both more effectively manifested, and more adequately recognized. At all times it is only an eye, capable of apprehending more than is conveyed by the channels of sense, that is able to discern it.

---

[1] Ps. xxiv. 7, Isa. xxvi. 15.   [2] Ps. lvii. 5, 11.
[3] Isa. xl. 4, 5: add lix. 19, lxvi. 18^b, 19^b, Ezek. xxxix. 13 ("get me glory"), 21.

Wherein, then, we may ask, does the world so reflect the Being of God as to be the expression of His glory? It is visible, firstly, in the fact, as such, of creation. I am not unaware of the debated ground which I am here touching. I am familiar with the maxim which beyond question is justified by all that experience teaches, *Ex nihilo nihil fit;* I recognize, moreover, that the idea cannot be conceived as a possible object of human science. But the very purport of Kant's celebrated treatment of the antinomies was to demonstrate, that human reason, abandoned to itself, could but oscillate between two equally inconceivable alternatives, and that to claim as possible an experiential knowledge of either was self-delusion. A belief, however, not derived from experience, or claimed as verifiable by it, is not excluded by the argument of Kant, even if that thinker do not expressly affirm it.[1] It may, therefore, in this connection, be not presumptuous to question the finality of the verdict of experience. If a Divine mind exist at all, the conditions of its operation must differ infinitely from any which we are able to imagine; the endeavour, therefore, to limit it, either by the apparent necessities of human thought, or by the conditions of human experience, would seem to be illegitimate. The only limitations to which it can be conceived to be subject are the moral and logical limitations, which have been ever

---

[1] *Kritik der Reinen Vernunft*, p. 467 Hartenstein (= ii. 597 f. Max Müller). See also Caird's *Kant*, p. 661 f. (cf. p. 587 f.).

recognized by theology, and which are inherent in its own nature and are not imposed from without.[1] Those at least, who while not venturing to define the mode, are content to accept the fact, of the dependence of the visible universe upon a Divine Mind, may see in it the exercise of an august and sovereign prerogative, differentiating Him absolutely from the highest of His creatures, a manifestation of His nature not indeed adequate to, but worthy of, Himself. For we have no right to assume that a given created system is either absolutely perfect, or a fully adequate expression of the Divine Nature ; since

> " Colui, che volse il sesto
> Allo stremo del mondo, e dentro ad esso
> Distinse tanto occulto e manifesto,
>   Non poteo suo valor sì fare impresso
> In tutto l'universo, che il suo verbo
> Non rimanesse in infinito eccesso.[2]

But with this limitation we may see in creation a signal and palmary exhibition of supreme goodness ; and, while not presuming to scrutinize or discover in their totality the motives by which it was prompted, may trace in it the operation of that generous love which sought to communicate to other beings fragments of its own Divine life, and to call into existence creatures, some with capacities to enjoy the gift of life, others able to apprehend and reciprocate the love.

If, leaving the fact of creation, we contemplate, so

[1] Comp. Pearson, *On the Creed*, Art. vi., on the word "Almighty" (παντοδύναμος), fol. 286-9.
[2] *Paradiso*, xix. 40-45.

ISAIAH'S VISION. 37

far as we are able, the means by which an abode has been prepared for the reception of life and intelligence, is it the majestic scale upon which the process has been conceived and carried out, or the rare and subtle mechanism which sustains the world in every part, or the intrinsic adequacy and beauty of the results, which impresses us as the most commensurate expression of the Divine glory? Do we speculate, as our philosophers have done, upon the structure of the material elements of which the fabric of created things is built? Strange and surprising conclusions are obtained, which compel our wonder, and force us to admit how deeply and securely, in regions to which no microscope can penetrate, the foundations of the world have been laid.[1] Do we ask the nature of the process by which this earth has been fitted for the habitation of man? We no longer suppose, with our forefathers, that it was created substantially as we know it some 6000 years ago.[2] We can realize, however inadequately, the gigantic nature of the movements involved. We can understand how in its formation every star which we gaze upon in the firmament may have co-operated; the immeasurable vista opens to

[1] See Tait, *Recent Advances in Physical Science* (ed. 3, 1885), lectures xii. and xiii., "The Structure of Matter" (esp. pp. 319 f., 329); and (more recently) Sir William Thomson, *Popular Lectures and Addresses*, vol. i. (ed. 2, 1891), "The Constitution of Matter," p. 220 ff. (and elsewhere).

[2] So, for instance, Pearson, *On the Creed*, Art. i. at the end (fol. 68), affirms the creation of the world to have taken place "most certainly within not more than six, or at farthest seven, thousand years."

our eyes; we travel back through the unnumbered and innumerable ages, and though the brain reels and imagination fails, can discern, at least dimly, the mighty lathe revolving in the skies, and see, now and again, the mass of glowing vapour flung off which is to become some future sun, and watch it slowly changing shape, slowly aggregating, and afterwards casting off in its turn smaller masses, each destined to become in time a planet. And then, as our interest centres on one of these planets, we perceive it slowly cooling; the circumambient vapours condense and form a sea; barren and bleak for æons, we at length observe that the rocks under the waters are clad with lowly foliage, and lowly animals swarm in the deep; we look again, and the land is covered with things creeping innumerable; soon afterwards, for centuries, mighty forests come and go over the globe in seemingly endless succession, huge reptiles are stirring everywhere, and birds of varied song move in the air; we look again, and the earth begins to wear the appearance with which in its wilder parts we are even now familiar, animals and trees and flowers much as we know them are visible; at length, —but who shall say Where? or When? — man appears, and the drama in the midst—or shall we say at the beginning?—of which we are actors ourselves begins to unfold itself before us. The magnitude and duration of the movements which have resulted in the formation of our earth, no imagination can grasp; the multitudinous variety of living organisms which

ISAIAH'S VISION. 39

in the æons that have passed have peopled it, no tongue can describe; the prodigality of resource which has endowed this life with the capacity of adapting, or, if you will, of transforming itself, in harmony with the varying conditions of its environment, no science can presume to gauge. Hardly more than twenty-five years ago one of our foremost naturalists [1] ventured to define for the ocean a zero of life, below which, as he supposed, living forms could not subsist; but since then the secrets of the deep have been disclosed, and its furthest recesses are known now to be astir with living creatures who find in its gloomy caverns a congenial home. I am not engaged to-day in arguing upwards, by any of the well-known methods, from the phenomena of nature to the existence of a Creator; but few will have the courage to deny that, if our belief in creation be well-founded, that which I have here faintly adumbrated would be a noble and worthy manifestation of the Creator's Being.

But this life, of which I have spoken, whence is it? what is it? Our definitions do but define the conditions which are observed to accompany it; they do not unlock the secret of that subtle combination of a few simple elements from which it results, or unveil the mystery of the unifying principle, which correlates, as mechanical or chemical forces do not correlate,

---

[1] Professor Edward Forbes. See Wyville Thomson's *Depths of the Sea*, pp. 5, 17 f.; or the *Report of the Challenger*, with the plates, esp. vol. i. pp. 33-50.

the several parts of a living organism, and welds them into a self-contained whole. Life without sensation, as we may presume it to exist in plants, is marvellous ; life with sensation, implying the presence of something which can translate the physical vibration coursing along the substance of a nerve into a felt pleasure or pain, is yet more so ; though the climax, most marvellous of all, is only reached when life is the exponent of a self-conscious personality, able not to feel only but to reflect, not to rest immersed in the needs or sensations of the moment, but to inquire, to speculate, to originate, to design ; not bounded by the present, but conscious that it stands related to a prodigious past, to an incalculable future ; possessing power to conceive and project ideals transcending every limitation of sense, proclaiming with a persistency that will not be denied the hidden links connecting it with a supersensuous world. In the formation, not of a dead material universe, but of a universe adapted, in at least one stage of its history, to support living forms, organized with this lavish profusion, and gifted with all the varied capacities which life implies, is it an illusion to see reflected that intense and inexpressible life which with undiminished potency and fulness energizes eternally in the Divine Mind?

But there is beauty in nature. True, beauty is a relative term : the symmetry which we admire in a leaflet or flower, the delicate gradations of tint to which a landscape owes its charm, alike imply the presence of an eye able to recognize and admire. Nevertheless, beauty exists for us; and we, who discern it, cannot pass it by. True, again, the harmonious disposition of form and colour which we term beauty, is not something superadded to nature: it is inherent in it. The iridescent colours on this insect's wing, the exquisite delicacy of that tiny bloom, the graceful convolutions of this fragile shell, the glittering brightness with which a winter's morning decks the forest, the changing hues which mark the steps of the declining year, the flood of splendour which in time of summer lights up the springing verdure in fields and meadows, and presently, as night approaches, suffuses the sky with a crimson glow—are, doubtless, one and all, the necessary consequences of a few optical and other physical laws. That is true: but it is not the entire truth. In nature, as in art, the more perfect the beauty, the more complex the means by which it is produced. The simplest form of natural beauty implies the co-operation of an indefinite multitude of distinct factors. Beauty, on its physical side, is an adjustment, a resultant from the combination of a practically infinite number of minute elements, effected by mechanism the most delicate, by agencies the most subtle, an adjustment of which the determining conditions were fixed in the bosom of eternity. If there be any truth in the teachings of science, the beauty which entrances our gaze to-day was implicit in the substance of the earth, as it was formed in the remote and incalculable past. That the disposition of natural substances and agencies which have been subservient to the maintenance and development of life upon the earth should in producing these effects have also produced what gratifies and impresses an intelligence contemplating them, is a remarkable and astonishing result. With admirable art, the mechanism of nature weaves, as it works, a web of beauty; and the curtain which it might have been feared would hide her rarest works of skill, in fact displays them. Nature is a picture which speaks to all, but most effectively, perhaps, to those who have reflected somewhat upon the secret processes of which her works are the visible result. Her resplendent colours, her rich and noble tapestry, are a vesture worthy of Him, whose form is hidden from mortal eyes, but whose presence is declared, as in Isaiah's vision, by the robe of state pendant from the heavenly throne.

But can we trace any evidence of the moral character of God? or is the earth full merely of the tokens of His power? Surely we cannot be mistaken in tracing evidence of the former in the constitution of human nature, in the affections and aspirations which it displays, in the conditions upon which social life is observed to depend. However it may be accounted for, it remains as a fact that human beings, organized as societies, have developed instincts for goodness, have practised and esteemed such virtues as kindness, benevolence, disinterestedness, justice. Partial and rudimentary within the narrow circle of

ISAIAH'S VISION. 43

the tribe, these affections expand and are confirmed as more settled habits are attained; limited here to one particular race, they are elsewhere extended to embrace mankind at large. We cannot ignore the fact of Christianity, even while we make no assumptions as to its origin or claims. Did we do so, that majestic "ethical monotheism," which has been assigned by the most searching of critics as the minimum of the prophets' teaching, would rise up and condemn us.[1] It is difficult to think that any theory of the origin of these sentiments, except indeed such as either merely restate in abstract but imposing phraseology the problem to be solved, or virtually deny that there are phenomena to be explained at all, can affect the evidence which they afford. Do we see in them, for example, an expansion and generalization of the "sympathetic desires" entertained by primitive man for his family, his friends, his clan? Then in the primitive human heart there was still implicit the same sentiment, under simpler conditions, of which we are conscious as active in ourselves. Do we see in our impulses to goodness the transformed instincts of self-preservation which we inherit from the ages during which our race was slowly maturing? Then it is implied, unless the dangerous metaphor of transformation deceives us, that human nature is not solely receptive, but superadds to a certain class of judgments an element

[1] Kuenen, *The Prophets and Prophecy in Israel* (1877), p. 589 ff.; cf. the same author's *Hibbert Lectures*, 1882, pp. 114-125.

not derived from experience. In either case, our moral preference is real, it is not merely a disguised self-interest; and its evidence is unimpeachable. It will not be out of harmony with the general order of nature, if our moral sensibilities have been gradually quickened; we only demand that the factors required to produce the results should be conceded explicitly at the beginning, and not surreptitiously introduced *at some point or other* of the process by which a moral and intelligible world is conceived to have arisen, and afterwards repudiated.[1] Until it has been shown, more conclusively than has yet been done, that when we seem to be exercising a virtue we are actually obeying an unreasoning necessity, or are entangled in the ruses of an Unconscious Will,[2] we must see in our moral judgments a reflection of the character of Him to whom the faculty by which we form them is itself due. He who has inspired human nature with true impulses of justice and generosity, of sympathy and love, with admiration for the heroic and the noble, with scorn for the ignoble and the mean, cannot but be possessed of a kindred character Himself.[3] He could not have constituted an intelligence that should admire, and strive to realize, attributes not inherent in Himself. Be it that conscience in certain savage tribes has remained undeveloped, be it that in other

---

[1] On the theories of ethics just referred to, comp. W. L. Courtney, *Constructive Ethics* (1886), pp. 228-277.

[2] Comp. *ibid.* pp. 278-318.

[3] Comp. Dr. Chalmers, *Bridgewater Treatise*, part i., chap. x., § 11 (= *Natural Theology*, book iv., chap. vi., § 11.

cases it is moulded by the habits, or reflects the temper, of society around, it is the capacity to acquire a conscience at all, whose decisions tend uniformly in one direction, which is the "witness of the soul" to God, speaking not less eloquently now than when, long ago, it was invoked by the African apologist against the polytheism and materialism of antiquity. Though the rays are broken, and the image is obscured, the moral glory of the Creator shines in the world: it is reflected in the verdict of the individual conscience; it is latent in the ethical sanctions upon which the permanence and welfare of society depends.

But these, it will be said, are the illusions of a superficial optimism. There are facts which neutralize the conclusions thus confidently drawn. Nature herself is inconsiderate and cruel. The life of one creature means the death, perhaps the painful death, of many others. Human existence has its ills, not less than its pleasures. Suffering surrounds us upon all sides. Here it is some disease which creeps insidiously into the frame, prostrates it for years upon a couch of pain, or cuts it off in the prime of youth and promise. There it is some deed of treachery or wrong, which deprives the weak of their right, and embitters the cup of life. Once it may have been the arbitrary will of a despot, or hard and barbaric habits of life: now it may be some galling link in the chain of social slavery, or the inexorable tyranny of competition. The question thus opened can here, it is evident, be touched on but cursorily. Doubtless the difficulty which such facts occasion can only be partially removed. Such facts excite our compassion: they move our pity: they kindle our resentment: they stimulate in us the very feelings to whose evidence we have just been appealing: they cannot silence the witness that we have already found. As regards moral evil it will be sufficient for the present argument to say that it has its source in the human will, operating admittedly in antagonism to the will of God, and in abuse of its gift of freedom. The whole mystery of pain cannot be solved: death, and violent death, was active upon this globe ages before our race was seen upon it. But looking at the brute creation by itself, we cannot say that the capacity for pain is not a necessary condition of the physical structure which animals possess, and of the capacity for enjoyment which in their case, as seems probable, immeasurably preponderates over pain. A thousand ties of interest or affection bind us to life, a thousand fears bid us shrink from death: of all these the animal creation is unconscious: what to it is the poignancy and bitterness of the grave? Nor, again, is pain wholly an evil: it is a means to an end: to the individual it is a preservative from danger: it has been an instrument in the formation and improvement of the race.[1] If, again, we consider the lower animals

[1] Comp. further on this subject, F. A. Dixey, "The Necessity of Pain," in No. xix. of the *Oxford House Papers* (Rivingtons, London, 1888); and the third Essay in *Lux Mundi* on "The Problem of Pain," by J. R. Illingworth.

as affected by the intervention of man, undoubtedly their sufferings have been increased thereby; but while the use made of them is legitimate, it is not more than an extension of that economy by which one part of nature is dependent upon another : where it is not legitimate, it results from an abuse of human power, and stands upon the same ground as other wrongs which have their source in a depraved human will.

If, lastly, we look at society, the ills which are indeed sadly patent in it must be admitted, even by an opponent, to be due largely to causes, the operation of which might be at once neutralized by the most ordinary exercise of forethought and thrift. Labour, exertion is not an evil : it braces and strengthens the character : to be relieved of the necessity of labour, either mental or bodily, though sometimes anticipated as the highest of blessings, is more often nothing less than a curse. In other cases physical evil is a result of human wrong-doing; and in so far as it has thus a tendency to prevent or punish sin, is a declaration that God is not merely benevolent, but that His benevolence is limited and guided by righteousness. Suffering which cannot be regarded as a consequence of sin, whether it comes in the form of accident or disease, or in one of the countless ways in which the innocent are entangled in the misdoings of the guilty, may partly have a moral, disciplinary value, and partly results from the operation of general laws, the suspension of which in individual cases could not be reasonably demanded, and would involve, if it were permitted, irremediable disorder. Nor, if the teaching of Christianity be true, can it be objected that the Creator watches with indifference either misery or sin. We can but suggest, with hesitation and trembling, partial alleviations of the difficulty. Either no reason higher than our own exists in the universe, in which case the facts of human reason itself are inexplicable; or there is a reason higher than our own, and in this case it seems incredible that the moral susceptibilities of the creature can be keener or truer than those of its Maker. The inference to which the dilemma points is that the source of the difficulty lies in our imperfect apprehension of the entire plan of creation. And yet, until we have apprehended this, and then found that the difficulty admits of no rational explanation, the positive evidence which we have obtained is not to be gainsaid. The result of modern scientific research has been indefinitely to enlarge and strengthen our conception of the solidarity of nature. In the interdependence here, in the correlation there, of widely separated parts, we trace unmistakably the expression of a comprehensive and deeply laid plan. If these are the characteristics of nature, viewed under its physical aspect, it is not unreasonable to expect similar characteristics in the phenomena of conscious life. There is much that we still see darkly and imperfectly: wisdom counsels us to trust, as analogy persuades us to believe, that in the light of a truer perspective, the anomalies which perplex us would disappear. Let us be grateful to those Hebrew prophets, whose visions have shown us glimpses of an unseen world, and whose intuitions have pierced where reason could never have hoped to reach. They have left reason abundant scope for speculation; but they have ennobled for us nature and history: they have irradiated the darkness that must otherwise have hung about our steps. Let us appropriate and seek to realize the few but pregnant words of the seraph's hymn, whose echoes are so familiar to us, and let our own voices unite with the celestial chorus, "Holy, Holy, Holy, is the LORD of Hosts: the fulness of the whole earth is his glory."

SERMON III.[1]

THE IDEALS OF THE PROPHETS.

Gen. xii. 3: "And I will bless them that bless thee, and him that curseth thee will I curse: and through thee shall all the families of the earth be blessed."

A DOUBLE stream of narrative runs through the first four Books of the Pentateuch. One of these, from the interest which it displays in the ceremonial institutions of Israel, may be conveniently termed the Priestly narrative; the other, conspicuous for its spiritual affinities with the writings of the canonical prophets, may be suitably described as the Prophetical narrative. In accordance with the mode of composition often followed by the Hebrew historical writers, the two narratives have been combined in our present Pentateuch: but the lines of demarcation between them are clearly definable; for in spirit, not less than in phraseology and style, they differ materially. The Priestly narrative culminates in the comprehensive view of the theocratic institutions, the Tabernacle, the priesthood, the sacrificial system,

[1] Preached at St. Mary's, before the University, on Sunday, Oct. 25, 1885.

contained in the three middle Books of the Pentateuch; in the preceding history only important occurrences, such as the Creation, or the covenants with Noah and Abraham, are described with minuteness, the narrative in other respects being brief, and limited to such details as would naturally be included in a historical introduction to the author's main subject. The Prophetical narrative, from which the popular view of the patriarchal and Mosaic period is mostly derived, exhibits to us the lives and doings of the patriarchs and their descendants, in a series of pictures, graphic in delineation, inimitable in literary form, and evincing a delicacy of touch and expression, a warmth of religious sympathy, and a keenness of moral and psychological perception, unsurpassed in the writings of the Old Testament. Expanded, elevated, and deepened, the spirit which animates the Prophetical narrative reappears in the noble and impressive eloquence of Deuteronomy. The theme of Deuteronomy is the observance, not as a law imposed from without, but as an intelligent and spontaneous expression of the heart, of the Decalogue and the Book of the Covenant which form an integral part of the Prophetical narrative in Exodus.[1]

[1] In support of the statements contained in the preceding paragraph, the writer may be permitted now to refer to his *Introduction to the Literature of the Old Testament* (ed. 3, 1892), especially pp. 109-114, 118-122, and (on Deuteronomy, and its relation to Ex. xx.-xxiii.), pp. 70-74, 91. The Decalogue (Ex. xx. 2-17) and "Book of the Covenant" (Ex. xx. 22—xxiii. 33 [see xxiv. 7]; cf. xxxiv. 10-26) form the foundation upon which the Deuteronomic legislation is constructed.

The text sets before us one of the characteristic features of the Prophetical narrative, that consciousness of the ideal destiny of Israel, which developed afterwards into the definite hope, commonly termed Messianic. Unfettered by the political and material limitations of his age, and looking beyond the horizon of his own time, the narrator discerns in dim outline the far-off goal of Israel's history, and enables his reader, with increasing clearness of vision, to discern it with him. Let me survey, rapidly, the stages in which he does this. The first is the familiar Protevangelion of the third chapter,[1] where hope already steps in to brighten the dark prospect, and alleviate the effects of the Fall, and where, though the struggle reserved for man may bring with it suffering and danger, and be protracted through uncounted generations, the issue, it is hinted, is not doubtful, but the seed of the woman will, in the end, prevail. Antagonism to evil is decreed to be the law of humanity; and though the nature of the influences prompting man to resist it, the course which the contest would take, and the manner in which the triumph would be finally secured, are not even remotely indicated, the outlook is one of promise and hope. We pass on, and come to Noah, the representative of the new humanity after the Flood, and his three sons typifying, the three great divisions of the human race with which the Hebrews were acquainted. The significance of the epoch is seized by the narrator; the broad differences of

[1] Gen. iii. 15.

THE IDEALS OF THE PROPHETS. 53

character stamped upon these nationalities are referred to the spell of the patriarchal blessing.[1] Obscure though the words are, we seem to see prefigured the expansive energy and many-sidedness of the nations of Europe, the political dependence and moral degradation of the populations of Canaan, and the blessedness of the people descended from Shem, on account of the light of religious truth shining in its midst. "Blessed be Jehovah, the God of Shem!" thus, expressively, is Shem designated as the most fortunate of the patriarch's sons; and it is within the limits of Shem's descendants that the seed of the woman must, if it is to be successful, carry on the conflict.

There follows the passage which I read as my text. It is typical of many, addressed sometimes to Abraham, sometimes to one of the other patriarchs. All breathe the same spirit; most are expressed nearly in the same words.[2] In part, the promises relate only to the nation of which the patriarchs are to be the ancestors; its numbers, as the stars of heaven, or as the sand which is upon the sea-shore; the certainty with which it will enter into possession of Canaan, even to the ideal limits reached by the dominion of Solomon;[3] the blessings of external prosperity which will flow to it. Elsewhere, a wider prospect is

[1] Gen. ix. 25-27.
[2] Gen. xii. 2-3, xiii. 14-17, xv. 5, 18, xviii. 18, xxii. 15-18 (Abraham); xxvi. 2-5, 24 (Isaac); xxvii. 27-29, xxviii. 13-15 (Jacob); xlix. 10 (Judah).
[3] Gen. xv. 18, cf. Ex. xxiii. 31; and see 1 Kings iv. 21. These passages explain the terms of the promise in Is. xxvii. 12.

opened, and the nations of the earth are brought within the sphere of Israel's influence. Three times, it is said,[1] through the patriarchs (or their seed) shall the families of the earth be blessed; twice,[2] in passages due perhaps to another hand, it is said that they will bless themselves by it, *i. e.* will own it as a source of good, and desire for themselves the blessings proceeding from it. Objectively, in other words, the truth of which Israel is the organ and channel is to become a blessing to the world; and subjectively, it is to be recognized by the world as such.[3] The thought in the latter case is one which becomes explicit in Isaiah, and may be illustrated from his vision of the nations urging one another to take part in the pilgrimage to Zion: "Come, and let us go up to the mountain of the LORD, for he will teach us out of his ways, and we will walk in his paths; for out of Zion shall go forth instruction, and the word of the LORD from Jerusalem."[4] The promises belonging to the Priestly narrative do not look so far. The Priestly narrative dwells upon important truths; it analyses the internal

---

[1] Gen. xii. 3, xviii. 18, xxviii. 14.
[2] Gen. xxii. 18, xxvi. 4.
[3] Comp. Riehm, *Messianic Prophecy* (ed. 2, Edinburgh, 1891), p. 97 f., who, however, interprets differently the three passages first cited, treating them—it must be admitted, in agreement with most modern scholars—as expressing the same sense as the two last quoted. Too much stress must not, therefore, be laid upon the distinction expressed in the text; though the fact of a different conjugation being used in the two sets of passages would seem to create a presumption in its favour. In illustration of the expression "bless *by*," see Gen. xlviii. 20 (R.V. *marg.*).
[4] Is. ii. 3.

THE IDEALS OF THE PROPHETS. 55

organization of the theocracy; it shows the significance of its ceremonial institutions; it formulates a conception of priesthood and sacrifice, destined to assume a central position in the ultimate phase of Israel's religion. In accordance with this, its general scope, the promises embodied in it are limited to Israel itself.[1] They emphasize the perpetuity of the relationship to be established between Israel and its God, and bring this into connection with their possession of the land of Canaan; but they nowhere contemplate the exertion by Israel of an influence upon the world without. On the other hand, the Prophetical narrative of the Pentateuch is inspired by that consciousness of a world-wide mission for Israel, which finds afterwards its more distinct and definite expression in the prophets.

What, we may ask, is the source of this conception of the ideal destiny of Israel, which thus prevails in so many parts of the Old Testament? Without committing ourselves to any theory of the growth of Hebrew historical literature, it seems possible to point to certain fundamental ideas, presupposed already in what have every appearance of being the oldest sources of the history, which may help us to answer the question. The song of Moses in Exodus xv., and that of Deborah in Judges v., attest for a period more ancient than that of the narrative in

---

[1] Gen. xvii. 6-8, xxxv. 11-12, Ex. vi. 2-8, xxix. 43-46. The two series of promises deserve to be compared with each other in detail.

which they are embedded,[1] the close relationship already regarded as subsisting between Israel and its God. They speak of the "people" of Jehovah, the people "claimed" and "purchased" by Him from bondage in Egypt, the people by whose deliverance the God of their ancestors had shown Himself to be the "strength and salvation" of their descendants.[2] Other ancient designations are the inheritance,[3] the possession,[4] the house [5] of Jehovah; or, in a more personal sense, His firstborn.[6] The idea of which different aspects are denoted under these figures is, doubtless, expressed most simply in the phrase first quoted, the people of Jehovah. At first, probably, it was not distinctly perceived that the God Who thus owned Israel's allegiance was also the Lord of the whole earth. Israel had its God, as other nations had their gods, whose real existence was scarcely denied.[7] But gradually it was seen what the expression involved, and when analysed, it was found to mean that the God of heaven and earth had really become Israel's God, had separated for Himself a particular nation in which to manifest His presence, and accomplish His purposes for mankind. Two passages in the Prophetical narrative of the Pentateuch exhibit this truth clearly. The first is the declaration

---

[1] See the writer's *Introduction*, pp. 27, 114, 161 f.
[2] Ex. xv. 2, 13 ("redeemed," more exactly "reclaimed"), 16ᵇ; Judg. v. 11ᵇ, cf. 23ᵇ.
[3] Ex. xv. 17, 1 Sam. xxvi. 19, 2 Sam. xiv. 16, xx. 19.
[4] Ex. xix. 5.   [5] Num. xii. 7.   [6] Ex. iv. 22.
[7] Ex. xv. 11, 1 Sam. xxvi. 19, Judg. xi. 24.

THE IDEALS OF THE PROPHETS. 57

to Abraham, so strangely and unfortunately mis-rendered in the Authorized Version,[1] "Shall I hide from Abraham that which I do . . . For I have known him, to the end that he may command his children and household after him, that they may keep the way of the LORD, to do justice and judgment?" Jehovah declares here that He has entered into a special relation with Abraham, in order to convey to him a fuller knowledge of His ways, which he may pass on to his descendants. The other passage is in the description of the consecration of the nation at Sinai:[2] "Now, therefore, if ye will obey my voice indeed, and keep my covenant, then ye shall be a peculiar treasure to me from among all peoples; for all the earth is mine; and ye shall be unto me a kingdom of priests, and an holy nation." Because the whole earth is Jehovah's, and His choice, therefore, is unrestricted, Israel is chosen by Him out of, and in preference to, all other nations, to enjoy the privilege of His ownership and protection; as we may venture to suppose, chosen not arbitrarily, but because in genius and temper it was best fitted to realize God's purposes towards man, to be the channel of His grace, and to develop, through many failures, an ideal of godliness and faith. Only, as is obvious, since Jehovah is a jealous God, and makes moral demands of His worshippers, this relation involves reciprocal obligations and responsibilities, on which, however, I have no occasion at present to dwell.

[1] Gen. xviii. 17, 19. [2] Ex. xix. 5-6.

Israel is the people of God; here is the fruitful germ of their entire future. The whole earth is the Lord's; and therefore, as the same prophetical narrator anticipates, it must in the end "be filled with his glory,"[1] and through Israel's intervention all flesh shall be brought to the knowledge of His salvation. We see the prophets of Israel, almost from the earliest times, in possession of ideas which are, so to speak, naturally expansive, which point to realities beyond themselves, and which imply logically the removal of the limitations which for the time confine them. The earliest records of the Old Testament are pregnant with the auguries of a noble future; they are inspired by the consciousness of an ideal at first discerned dimly and in outline, afterwards defined more accurately, an ideal moreover which, as history proceeded, so far from proving itself an illusion, or an impracticable vision, was actually, more or less completely, realized. Let us follow, in some of its more salient aspects, its development.

The establishment of the monarchy forms an epoch in Israelitish history. The monarchy created in Israel a sense of national unity, and gave a new impulse to national feeling, which though soon indeed ruptured, never ceased to be remembered, and left its mark upon the whole subsequent history. David and Solomon secured for Judah, in particular, a prestige and a pre-eminence which never afterwards forsook it. The nation culminated in its monarch;

[1] Num. xiv. 21.

THE IDEALS OF THE PROPHETS. 59

its aims and aspirations became his; he was the permanent centre by which its different parts were held together, and the welfare of the whole was maintained. Instituted under the favour and approval of God,[1] his earliest title is "Jehovah's Anointed one";[2] his position is unique; in defending his country's cause he fights the "battles of Jehovah";[3] his person is sacred—"Who will put forth his hand against the Lord's Anointed, and be guiltless?"[4] As representative of the nation, the hopes fixed upon the nation are transferred to him; prophets announce to him a glorious future, poets make him their theme; his figure is idealized, and the portrait of the Messianic King is before us. This, however, was only attained gradually; let us trace the steps in detail. The substance, if not the exact words, of the momentous announcement made to David by Nathan[5] is doubtless correctly preserved. To his successor, Israel's own title of son is solemnly attached;[6] the perpetuity of his dynasty is promised; though temporarily disgraced it will not be permanently set aside; the future of Israel's existence is definitely associated with Israel's king.[7] The thought is repeated in David's beautiful "Last Words,"[8] in which, after

[1] 1 Sam. ix. 15 f., x. 1.
[2] 1 Sam. xvi. 6, xxiv. 6, 10, xxvi. 9, 16, 2 Sam. xix. 22.
[3] 1 Sam. xviii. 17, xxv. 28.
[4] 1 Sam. xxvi. 9; cf. xxiv. 6, 2 Sam. i. 14, 16.
[5] 2 Sam. vii. 4-16.
[6] 2 Sam. vii. 14 (cf. the quotation in Ps. lxxxix. 26 f.): see Ex. iv. 22 f., Hos. xi. 1.
[7] 2 Sam. vii. 14-16.   [8] 2 Sam. xxiii. 1-7.

dwelling on the blessings of a just rule, he expresses his confidence in the future reserved for his own house. In these passages are drawn the first lineaments of the features which were afterwards more fully developed in the Messianic Psalms.

The great prophets amplify in different directions the thought of Israel's ideal future. I will select three typical illustrations of this. Amos prophesied in the Northern Kingdom towards the middle of the 8th century B.C., and was the first, so far as we know, to point out to his countrymen the determining influence soon to be exerted by the Assyrians upon the history of Western Asia.[1] Amos rudely shatters the illusions of security cherished by the proud citizens of Samaria.[2] Appropriating the words of the prophetical narrator of Genesis, he gives them an unexpected and startling application: "You only have I known of all the families of the earth: therefore will I visit upon you all your iniquities."[3] But while declaring the certainty of approaching evil and disgrace, his prophecy does not close without a reservation; the chosen people cannot be entirely cast off; the nation, though the vision of woe seemed to threaten it with extinction, is only sifted, so that no sound grain falls to the earth.[4] The breach which the empire of David had lately sustained will be healed,[5] and its power re-established to its

---

[1] Amos vi. 14.
[2] See Amos v. 18-20, vi. 1-7, 13, ix. 10^b.
[3] Amos iii. 2; see Gen. xviii. 18, 19.
[4] Amos ix. 8-10.
[5] Amos ix. 11; see 2 Kings xiv. 13.

THE IDEALS OF THE PROPHETS. 61

old limits.[1] Amos substantially renews and re-asserts the promise of Nathan; the re-elevation of David's weakened house, the restoration to Israel of material prosperity, are the aspects of the future upon which his thoughts rest.

We come to Isaiah, who in the prophecies inspired by the great crises through which he saw his country pass, gives brilliant and distinct expression to Israel's hope. He develops it in three directions. First, he anticipates for his people the speedy advent of an ideal future, when the nation, purified, regenerated, transformed, will be true to its ideal character, and realize its ideal aims. In Exodus we read, "And ye shall be unto me a kingdom of priests, and an holy nation":[2] Isaiah writes, "And he that is left in Zion, and he that remaineth in Jerusalem, shall be called holy"; and in imagery drawn from the narrative of the Pentateuch, he depicts the supernatural splendour which will rest as a canopy and defence over the sacred city.[3] Again and again is the thought, with a wealth and variety of imagery, which only Isaiah can command, reiterated; again

---

[1] Amos ix. 12. The allusion is to the nations which David had subjugated (2 Sam. viii.), and "over which," in consequence, Jehovah's "name had been called" in token of ownership (see, in illustration of this expression, 2 Sam. xii. 28, R.V. *marg.*, Deut. xxviii. 10, 1 Kings viii. 43, Jer. vii. 10, 11, xxv. 29. In the English Bible the phrase is usually rendered, obscurely and inexactly, "called by my name," but the correct rendering is sometimes given on the margin of the Revised Version, *e.g.* in Jer. vii. 10).

[2] Ex. xix. 6.   [3] Is. iv. 3, 5, 6.

and again do we linger on those marvellous pictures of serenity, purity, and peace, which are the creations of his inspired imagination.[1] And it is not solely, or even primarily, the return of material prosperity upon which his interest is fixed; it is the future in its spiritual aspects, the regeneration of the people, its conformity to its ideal character, which is the conspicuous and central feature in nearly every picture which he draws.

Here, then, is one aspect of the future, as conceived by Isaiah. A second aspect is connected directly with the promise of Nathan. In lieu of the mere permanence of the Davidic dynasty, in lieu of the abstract figure of David, under whom Hosea declares that the broken unity of the nation will be repaired,[2] Isaiah sets before us the concrete personality of the Messianic King. We can follow the stages by which the idea took shape in his mind. First, on occasion of that memorable interview with Ahaz, when, after the sullen repulse of his offer by the king, there rises before his mental eye, as it would seem without premeditation, the vision of the maiden, soon to give birth to the child, who, in spite of the destitution through which his country must first pass, is still the mysterious pledge and symbol of its deliverance.[3]

---

[1] See, for instance, Is. i. 26-27, xxx. 19-26, xxxii. 1-8, 15-18, xxxiii. 20, 21.

[2] Hos. iii. 5.

[3] Is. vii. 14-16. The destitution is indicated by the simple fare of "curdled milk and honey," to which the child (vii. 15), not less than the people generally (vii. 21 f.), will be reduced.

THE IDEALS OF THE PROPHETS. 63

A year or more passes by :[1] again the prophet is discoursing on the political prospects of his country ; he is watching the torrent of Assyrian invasion, as it inundates the Northern Kingdom ; he sees it sweeping impetuously onward into Judah ; it threatens to submerge all ; it has already risen to the neck—" and the stretching out of his wings shall fill the breadth of thy land, O Immanuel !" No sooner does the magic word escape the prophet's lips, than his tone instantly changes; the torrent melts away: he challenges, defiantly, the combined nations, distant or near, and with a burst of triumph, announces their overthrow.[2] Can clearer proof be needed, how vividly the prophet realizes the unborn child of his imagination, or with what august attributes he conceives him to be endowed ? And at the end of the same section, when the clouds which darken the political horizon have finally lifted, and a morning of hope and joy breaks upon the restored people, we see the child, invested with every attribute of an ideal prince, ruling in David's seat, and inaugurating a reign of peace : " For all the armour of the armed men in the tumult, and the garments rolled in blood, shall be for burning, for fuel of fire. For a child is born unto us, a son is given unto us ; and the government is upon his shoulder ; and his name is called, Wonderful Counsellor, Mighty God, Everlasting Father, Prince of Peace."[3] Nor is this all. Twenty, or, more

[1] Is. viii. 1-4.   [2] Is. viii. 7-10.
[3] Is. ix. 5-7 (the end of the section which begins at viii. 5).

SERMON III.

probably, thirty[1] years afterwards, when the army of Sennacherib, having reduced, one after another, his rebellious vassals in Phœnicia, is starting southwards to wreak upon Jerusalem a like fate, the prophet, having in a passage of unsurpassed irony and power[2] declared his failure, proceeds to that unique delineation of the Messianic age,[3] which has been pronounced, not unjustly,[4] to be perhaps the most remarkable creation of pre-Christian times. Again the prince of David's line is set before us, endowed by the spirit of Jehovah with a threefold gift, with the faculty of quick and true perception, with strength alike in deliberation and action, with profound religious intuitions, delicate and acute in discrimination, sagacious in judgment, effecting by the breath of his mouth—a wonderful image—what ordinary rulers would only accomplish by physical coercion, transforming the wild passions of human nature, and finally, by the moral attractiveness of his own personality, riveting the attention and interest of the

---

[1] The capture of Damascus, foretold in Is. viii. 4, is fixed by the Inscriptions for B.C. 732 ; and the deportation of the inhabitants of Zebulun, Naphtali, &c. (2 Kings xv. 29), alluded to in Is. ix. 1, took place B.C. 734 : the date of vii. 1—ix. 7 will thus be c. B.C. 735-34. Sennacherib's invasion, to the period of which x. 5—xii. seems to the present writer to belong, took place in B.C. 701 : even, however, should this prophecy, as Dillmann, for instance, supposes, belong to the reign of Sargon, it will still be subsequent to B.C. 722, and thus many years later than vii. 1—ix. 7.
[2] Is. x. 28-34.   [3] Is. xi. 1-10.
[4] Duhm, *Theologie der Propheten* (1875), p. 168.

THE IDEALS OF THE PROPHETS. 65

world. It is important to bear in mind the chronology (where it can be ascertained) of Isaiah's prophecies; for it assists us to understand the true nature of his ideas. It shows us that though attached in one sense to contemporary occurrences, they are in another sense independent of time. They reappear in a new and more developed form after the occasion out of which they arose had passed by: they form part of his permanent intellectual creed; though he seems to expect for them an immediate realization, the postponement, so far from destroying his hopes, invigorates and renews them. From the prospect of his nation's ideal future, sometimes with, sometimes without, the central figure of the ideal King, he draws, in the days of his country's sorest trial, consolation and strength.[1]

A third feature in Isaiah's conception of the future attaches itself immediately to the thought expressed in the text. He has a vivid consciousness of the position to be ultimately assumed in the world by the religion of Israel. He contemplates, not merely, like Amos, the enforced subjection of the neighbouring nations to David's successors; he contemplates the homage and allegiance offered by them spontaneously to Israel's faith. In the passage from one of his earliest prophecies which I have already quoted, he represents to us the nations streaming to Zion as their spiritual metropolis; and later he views in succession one nation after another, Moab, Ethiopia,

[1] *E.g.* Is. ix. 1-7, xxix. 20-24, xxx. 19-26, xxxiii. 5, 6, 13-24.

Egypt, Tyre,[1] incorporated in the future kingdom of God. The thought is most distinctly expressed in his prophecy on Egypt: not only are the symbols of Jehovah's worship established in that country, but there is a highway between Egypt and Assyria, and the two nations, engaged then in deadly hostility, pass freely together along it, doing homage with Israel itself to Israel's God.[2]

Such are the three principal developments which the truth of Israel's future received in Isaiah's hands. He delineates with a distinctness and emphasis unknown before its ethical characteristics; he exhibits in its completeness (for subsequent prophets added but little to it) the portrait of the ideal King; and he insists, with a generous and far-seeing catholicity, upon the essential universalism of the national faith.

My third typical illustration is drawn from the great prophecy of Israel's restoration, which occupies the last twenty-seven chapters of the Book of Isaiah. Here Israel's future is conceived under an entirely new aspect. The figure of the Messianic King is absent, and there appears instead the figure of the ideal nation. Israel, no longer viewed as an aggregate of isolated members, but grasped as a whole, is dramatized as an individual, in whom the essential characteristics of the people are concentrated, and who stands before us realizing in his own person its purposes and aims. The basis of the personification

---

[1] Is. ii. 2-4, xvi. 4-5, xviii. 7, xix. 19-25, xxiii. 18.
[2] Is. xix. 23.

THE IDEALS OF THE PROPHETS. 67

is the prophetic office of the nation. Israel has been called of God in its ancestor Abraham, has received from Him a definite commission and work, and is now honoured by Him with the title, implying trust and confidence on the one side, devotion and loyalty on the other, of His servant.[1] The conception thus formed is not, however, limited to the representation of Israel, as it was in the past; it is invested by the prophet with an independent being, and projected by him, as a truly ideal form, upon the future. And so vivid is the personification, that it assumes the character of an Individual, who reproduces in his own person the salient characteristics of the nation. This individual has a mission, not to his own people merely, but to the world: "It is a small thing that thou shouldest be my servant to raise up the tribes of Jacob, and to restore the preserved of Israel; I will also give thee for a light to the Gentiles, that my salvation may be even unto the ends of the earth."[2] He is thus the instrument for communicating the truth possessed by Israel to the world. In his work as prophet, he will encounter contumely and opposition: but he will not flinch; the mystery of suffering must be exemplified in him; and though innocent himself, he will sacrifice his life for the relief and benefit of others. But this is not the end. He lives again, a new and glorified life, in which the travail of his soul is no longer unrewarded; his work prospers

[1] Is. xli. 8-10, xliii. 1-2, xliv. 1, 2.
[2] Is. xlix. 6 (cf. xlii. 6-7).

SERMON III.

in his hands; he takes his place beside the great ones of the earth, and whereas before all were shocked at the sight of his humiliation, the world itself will now stand amazed at the spectacle of his exaltation.[1] Israel, as the recipient of prophetic illumination, and the bearer of a message to mankind, is here concentrated in an ideal figure, who exhibits in their perfection the typical excellences of the nation, and realizes in their integrity its ideal aims. Nor is it an abstract character which the prophet thus depicts; his own warmth of feeling and imaginative sympathy are reflected in it; it is human in its completeness; it speaks in accents of sweetness and pathos; it shows no deficiency in strength and decision,[2] yet the attributes of sympathy, tenderness, and resignation predominate;[3] for a moment it is disheartened, but is quickly re-assured;[4] unobtrusively but surely it accomplishes its ends.[5] Such is the personality upon which, in the mind of the great prophet of the exile, the future alike of Israel and the world depends.[6]

These, then, are a few of those auguries of the

[1] Is. xlii. 1-7, xlix. 1-9, l. 4-9, lii. 13—liii. 12.
[2] Is. l. 7 f.   [3] lxi. 1—3, liii. 7.   [4] xlix. 4.   [5] xlii. 2-4.
[6] The thoughts expressed in this and the preceding paragraphs have been developed by the writer more fully in his volume, *Isaiah, his life and times, and the writings which bear his name*, in the series entitled *Men of the Bible:* comp. pp. 40-42, 94 f., 110-114, 175-180. On the figure of Jehovah's ideal servant (of which it is not easy to gain a perfectly consistent picture), much that is helpful and suggestive will be found in A. B. Davidson's study in the *Expositor*, 1884, Nov. p. 350 ff., Dec. p. 430 ff.; comp. also the remarks of Dillmann, in his commentary on Isaiah (1890), p. 472 f.

THE IDEALS OF THE PROPHETS. 69

future, which are the unique creation of the Hebrew prophets, and which through a succession of ages ministered to the consolation, and sustained the faith, of the Israelitish nation. Have they failed of their accomplishment? We, whose privilege it is to be born in the Messianic age, are witnesses of, at least, the initial stages of their fulfilment. In the Gospel the principles determining the history of Israel are unfolded and matured : it is upon this larger and firmer ground, and not by the fragile aid of doubtful or mistranslated texts, that the unity of the two Testaments is to be maintained. In the empire exercised by Christ over the minds of men, we recognize the transfigured kingdom of David. In the new life conferred by union with Him, in the gifts of the Spirit, as eloquently summed up by St. Paul,[1] we recognize that transformation of the individual character and of society, which formed Isaiah's inspiring ideal. By the diffusion of the faith of Christ throughout the world, the catholicity of the prophets' visions receives its justification. The very words of the commission addressed to St. Paul in the Acts, are borrowed from those in which the world-wide mission of the individualized people is described in the second part of Isaiah;[2] for in the work inaugurated by the Apostle of the Gentiles the " Righteous Servant" first accomplishes this part of his office. In His own life and sufferings, the Redeemer realizes the character

---

[1] Gal. iii. 22, 23, Col. iii. 12-14.
[2] Acts xiii. 47 ; Is. xlix. 6.

sketched, as I have endeavoured to show, with such completeness and power, in the same chapters; and the portrait which on the one hand reflects, as in a miniature, the best and truest features of the Israelitish nation, is, on the other hand, found to be a prefigurement of the human personality of Christ. In the fulfilment it was seen how the two characters, that of the ideal King, or Messiah, and that of the ideal Prophet or Sufferer—which are distinct, and never approximate, in the Old Testament,—could be combined in one person.[1] In Christ as King, and Christ as Prophet, the Founder and Head of a new social state—for the aspects of His work as Priest would carry me too far to-day—the hope of Israel, which but for His advent, had been as an illusion or a dream, finds its consummation and its reward.

But the change was neither so rapid nor so complete as the prophets themselves seem to have expected. Long centuries passed, and Israel seemed on the verge of extinction, before the Child who, as Isaiah and Micah represent, was to save his country from Assyria, appeared. In particular the transformation of human life remains still a potentiality not realized. Even where the wheat appears to abound, the tares are mingled with it. Whether indeed it will ever be different while the present order of things continues upon earth we cannot say; the most dazzling visions of the prophets are indeed localized upon this earth; their centre is the earthly, though

[1] Comp. the writer's *Isaiah*, p. 180.

glorified, Zion:[1] but in the New Testament the vista ends elsewhere; and there only, perchance, their final consummation is to be sought. Let us endeavour by the grace of Christ, and in the light of His example, to realize the ideal as completely as we are able in ourselves. Let us, by maintaining and promoting, as well in the secular as the religious life—for both are comprehended in the Messianic ideal—an elevated standard of action, contribute as we can towards diffusing in the world the blessings which flow from the inheritance of Abraham.

[1] See, for instance, Is. iv. 3, 5, xxv. 6-8 ("in this mountain"), xxxiii. 20, 21, liv. 11-14, lx. 1-22, lxii. 1, Jer. iii. 14 f., xxxiii. 16, Ezek. xlviii. 35, &c. Comp. Prof. A. B. Davidson's *Ezekiel*, pp. 288-90.

SERMON IV.[1]

GROWTH OF BELIEF IN A FUTURE STATE.

2 Tim. i. 10: "Who abolished death, and brought life and incorruption to light through the Gospel."

I PROPOSE to take as my subject this afternoon the doctrine of a future state, as it was current in Jewish circles, before, and immediately following, the Christian era. I shall, firstly, exhibit, as time will permit, the eschatology of our main pre-Christian authority, the apocryphal Book of Enoch: I shall, secondly, exemplify the eschatological interpretation of the Old Testament, from the Jewish Targums; and, in conclusion, I shall consider briefly the results thus obtained in their bearing upon the teaching of the New Testament.

I may be permitted to premise shortly, what I should have been glad to develop at length, the stages through which the doctrine had passed before the close of the Old Testament canon. The ordinary

---

[1] Preached at St. Mary's, on Sunday, March 6, 1887, being one of the sermons, preached annually before the University, on the foundation of the late Dr. Macbride, Principal of Magdalen Hall, and Lord Almoner's Professor of Arabic, upon "The Jewish Interpretation of Prophecy."

GROWTH OF BELIEF IN A FUTURE STATE. 73

belief on the subject of a future life, shared by the ancient Hebrews, was not that the spirit after death ceased to exist,[1] but that it passed into the underworld, Sheol, the "meeting-place," as Job describes it, "for all living,"[2] as well for the tyrant King of Babylon, at whose downfall the earth rejoiced,[3] as for Jacob, or Samuel, or David,[4] where it entered upon a shadowy, half-conscious existence, devoid of interest and occupation, and not worthy of the name of "life"[5] :—" For Sheol cannot praise thee, death cannot celebrate thee : they that go down into the pit cannot hope for thy faithfulness."[6] But the darkness which thus shrouded man's hereafter was not unbroken in the Old Testament ; and there are three lines along which the way is prepared for the fuller revelation brought by the Gospel. There is, firstly, the limitation of the power of death set forth by the prophets, in their visions of a glorified, but yet earthly, Zion of the future : " For as the days of a tree shall be the days of my people, and my chosen shall long enjoy the work of their hands."[7] There is, secondly, the conviction uttered by individual Psalmists that their close fellowship with God implies and demands that

---

[1] See, *e.g.* 1 Sam. xxviii. 15.   [2] Job xxx. 23.
[3] Is. xiv. 8, 9, 15 : comp. Ezek. xxxii. 18-32 : also Job iii. 13-19.
[4] Gen. xxxvii. 35 (see R.V. *marg.*, and cf. xliv. 29), 1 Sam. xxviii. 15, 2 Sam. xii. 23.
[5] See Note A (p. 95).
[6] Is. xxxviii. 18 (Hezekiah's song) : similarly Ps. vi. 5, xxx. 9, lxxxviii. 10-12, cxv. 17 ("The dead praise not Jah, neither any that go down into silence " : with " silence," comp. Ps. xciv. 17).
[7] See Note B (p. 95).

they will themselves personally be superior to death :
"My flesh and my heart faileth; but God is the
strength of my heart and my portion for ever."[1]
And, thirdly, we meet with the idea of a resurrection,
though rather at first as a hope than as a dogma, and
with the limitation that it is restricted to Israel.
"Let thy dead live! let my dead bodies arise!" cries
the dwindled nation in its extremity; and the
prophet forthwith utters the jubilant response:
"Awake and sing, ye that dwell in the dust; for thy
dew is as the dew of lights, and the earth shall cast
forth the Shades."[2] But the hope thus triumphantly
expressed is limited by the context to Israel;[3] and
the same limitation is apparent in the vision of the
dry bones in Ezekiel xxxvii.[4] Even in Dan. xii. 2,
the passage which speaks most distinctly, and teaches
also a resurrection of the wicked, the terms are still
not universal: "And many of them that sleep in the
dust of the earth shall awake, some to everlasting
life, and some to shame and everlasting contempt."[5]
But this verse adds, for the first time, the idea of a
future retribution, which also may be signified by the

[1] Ps. lxxiii. 26 (comp. *v.* 24^b); cf. xvi. 10 f. (R.V.), xvii. 15, xlix. 15 ; Job xix. 26. See the Commentary of Delitzsch on the passages from the Psalms, or Kirkpatrick, *The Psalms (Book I.)*, in the *Cambridge Bible for Schools*, p. lxxvii f. ; and A. B. Davidson's Commentary on Job (in the same series) *ad loc.*, and p. 291 ff.

[2] Is. xxvi. 19 (post-exilic). See Note C (p. 96).

[3] Observe that the *foes* of Israel are without hope of a resurrection (*v.* 14) : comp. Jer. li. 39, 57.

[4] See *v.* 11.   [5] See Note D (p. 96).

GROWTH OF BELIEF IN A FUTURE STATE. 75

"judgment," to which the Preacher, in Ecclesiastes, more than once solemnly alludes.[1]

Such is the point at which the Old Testament leaves the doctrine of a future life. I proceed to trace the main developments which the doctrine underwent at the hands of the Jews before the time of Christ. One feature which at once strikes us is that it is brought into an intimate connection with the developed doctrine of the Messiah, to which the same period gave birth. There is no passage in the Old Testament, in which such a connection is asserted, at least explicitly.[2] But in the centuries immediately preceding the Christian era, the Messianic idea assumed a new prominence, and was presented under fresh forms, among which were some professing an eschatological significance. When Judah fell under Greek influences, and morally as well as politically the supremacy of Hellenism began to assert itself, those who still remained faithful to the religion of their fathers found themselves engaged in a new struggle, now with aggressive irreligion without, now with religious indifferentism within.[3] Their hearts pondered over the ancient prophecies, so strangely unfulfilled, of Israel's future greatness and glory: from the sufferings and disappointments of the present, they turned to the prospects of their realization in the future; or sought for compensation in the hope of a glorified life hereafter. The Book of

[1] See Note E (p. 96). [2] See Note F (p. 97).
[3] See 1 Macc. i. 10-64.

SERMON IV.

Daniel is the first known literary work in which reflections such as these took shape:[1] but in the hands of subsequent writers the same mode of representation was developed in far greater detail. Taking as their basis the well-known prophecy of Daniel, which unites the figure of a super-human Messiah with the promise of a kingdom conferred upon the saints of the Most High,[2] these writers combined with it elements derived from other, more ancient, prophecies of the ideal future of their nation; they imagined the time when the heathen domination under which they laboured would be overthrown, and the power which it now wielded transferred to the people of God: under concrete images of wonderful attractiveness and force, they pictured the Messiah triumphing with His people over their foes, or presiding, as the vice-gerent of the Almighty, at the judgment of quick and dead. The germs of that mode of representation, known as the "Apocalyptic,"[3] appear in the writings of the earlier post-exilic prophets;[4] but set forth upon a scale designed to meet effectively the needs of the time, and to provide a satisfaction in the future for the hopes and expectations unaccomplished in the present,

---

[1] See, in particular, Dan. ii. 35, 44-45, ch. vii., viii., x.-xii. The book of Daniel appears to date from the beginning of the persecution of Antiochus Epiphanes: comp. the writer's *Introduction*, ch. ix., and, on its purport and aim, pp. 477-481.
[2] Dan. vii. 13 (R.V.), 14, 22, 27.
[3] See Note G (p. 97).
[4] Comp. Zech. i.-viii., xii.-xiv., Joel iii.

GROWTH OF BELIEF IN A FUTURE STATE. 77

it belongs essentially, as has been explained, to a later age.

The most remarkable and, next to the book of Daniel, the earliest example of this type of literature is the Apocalypse of Enoch. The Book of Enoch, as a whole, is known only through the medium of an Ethiopic version;[1] it is accessible now to English readers in the useful edition of Prof. Schodde.[2] Into critical questions connected with its structure, there is no occasion for me to enter: if it be not all the work of one hand, it breathes throughout the same spirit; and the elements composing it are assigned by the great majority of critics to the second and first centuries B.C.[3] Enoch, it is said, "walked with God"; and the book consists of a series of visions, or revelations, supposed to have been received by the patriarch, and opening to him the mysteries of the invisible world. The general scope of the book, the announcement, viz. of future judgment, is declared in the opening chapter, constructed largely upon

[1] Published first by Archbishop Laurence, from a MS. in the Bodleian Library, in 1838; and again, with a collation of other MSS., by Dillmann in 1851.

[2] Andover, U.S.A. (1882), with introduction and notes, based (naturally) upon what the author justly terms the standard edition (in German) of Dillmann (Leipzig, 1853). Laurence's translation (recently re-printed) is not always trustworthy. A new translation, with notes, embodying many various readings, from MSS. not known at the time when Dillmann's edition was published, is understood to be in preparation by the Rev. R. H. Charles.

[3] Schürer, *Gesch. des Jüd. Volkes im Zeitalter Jesu Christi*, ii. (1886), p. 620 f.

reminiscences of the prophets, and containing the passage cited in the Epistle of Jude.[1] There follows an account of the first great act of judgment, executed upon the rebel angels who seduced the daughters of men, and introduced upon earth the knowledge of corrupt arts. After this, Enoch, under the guidance of an angel, travels over various regions of the earth, and learns the secrets of nature, particularly such as stand related to the moral government of the world. The central part of the book, chapters 37—71, contain the sections which deal most directly with the final Messianic judgment, and describe the person and office of the Judge. In the closing chapters of the book, after a long allegorical description of the history of Israel, the author, addressing his contemporaries, sums up, in tones of fervour and moral earnestness, the practical lessons which his revelations suggest. This application of the belief in a future state, as a motive to action, marks the more advanced stage which the doctrine has reached. Nothing of the kind occurs in the pages of the Old Testament.

I may now describe the eschatology of the book. In the first part, we read chiefly of the fallen angels, and of their punishment; in accordance with the

[1] Jude 14-15. See Enoch i. 9: "And behold he cometh with ten thousands of holy ones, to execute judgment upon them; and he will destroy the ungodly, and contend with all flesh concerning all that the sinners and the godless have done against him and committed." Comp., for the elements on which the representation is based, Deut. xxxiii. 2, Jer. xxv. 31, Is. xvi. 16, Dan. vii. 10.

allusion in Jude,[1] they are represented as bound in chains and darkness, awaiting the judgment of the Great Day.[2] But we hear likewise of the abode in which the spirits of the departed pass the intermediate state; and in the far West, Enoch visits in his travels the fair and secluded resting-places reserved for the spirits of the righteous; and not far thence beholds those other places in which the souls of the wicked, in pain and woe, expect their final judgment.[3] Elsewhere, allusion is made to a "garden of righteousness," or "of the righteous,"[4] situate in the East, the relation of which to the abodes just described is not distinctly indicated, but which appears to be the prototype of what was afterwards known as the "Garden of Eden" (or "Paradise"), the abode of the faithful departed. Resuming his travels, Enoch is brought to the Holy City, Jerusalem, and notices beside it a deep and sterile valley. He inquires what it is, and what purpose it subserves. It is the valley of Hinnom, Gehinnom, better known under its Graecized name, Gehenna. "This," said the angel Uriel,[5] "this accursed valley is for those who will be accursed to eternity, and here will be assembled all those who have uttered with their mouths unseemly words against God, and spoken insolently of his glory; here will they be assembled, and here will be their judgment. And in the last days will the spectacle of a just judgment upon them be exhibited before the

---

[1] Jude 6.   [2] x. 5-6, 12-14.   [3] Ch. xxii.
[4] xxxii. 3, lxxvii. 3, lx. 8, 23, lxi. 12.   [5] Ch. xxvii.

righteous,[1] for ever and ever; and for this, will those who have obtained mercy bless the Lord of Glory, the Eternal King." Such is the earliest description of Gehenna, as a place of torment. The locality is not idealized: it is the actual valley beside Jerusalem; and the idea of the writer appears to be that while the Holy City will be the capital of the Messianic kingdom, the valley close at hand will be the perpetual scene of the punishment of the wicked. This idea is probably an extension of the thought expressed in the last verse of the book of Isaiah.[2]

The resurrection and future judgment are described principally in the visions in the central part of the book. I will quote some of the most characteristic passages. The resurrection is no longer confined to Israel, it is universal—"And[3] in those days Sheol will give back them that are entrusted to it, and Destruction will restore that which it owes. And he will choose from among them the just and the holy: for the day has come when they shall be delivered. And the Chosen One"—such is the title bestowed upon the Messiah—"in those days will sit upon his throne, and all the hidden things of wisdom will proceed from the thoughts of his mouth: for the Lord of spirits

---

[1] Cf. xlviii. 9, 10, lxii. 12.

[2] "And they (the pilgrims from all nations, visiting Jerusalem, v. 23) shall go forth, and look upon the carcases of the men that have transgressed against me: for their worm shall not die, neither shall their fire be quenched; and they shall be an abhorring unto all flesh."

[3] li. 1-3.

GROWTH OF BELIEF IN A FUTURE STATE. 81

has given it to him, and glorified him." "And[1] I saw one who had a head of days"—*i. e.* a head betokening age—"and his head was white like wool: and with him was another, whose countenance was as the appearance of a man, and his countenance was full of grace, as one of the holy angels. And I asked one of the angels who went with me, and who showed me all the hidden things concerning this son of man, who he was, and whence he came, and why he goeth with the Head of Days? And he answered and said unto me: This is the son of man, who hath justice, with whom righteousness dwells, and who reveals the treasures of all that is hidden, because the Lord of spirits hath chosen him, and whose portion before the Lord of spirits exceedeth all, by reason of righteousness, unto eternity. And this son of man, whom thou hast seen, will arouse kings and mighty men from their couches, and the strong from their thrones, and will loosen the bands of the strong, and break the teeth of the sinners. . . . And he will thrust aside the face of the strong, and shame shall cover them: darkness shall be their dwelling-place, and worms shall be their couch; neither shall they have any hope of arising from their couches, because they exalt not the name of the Lord of spirits." The deeds done in the flesh are inscribed in books,[2] which are opened on the day of final judgment—the "day of the great judgment," as it is termed [3]—before God

---

[1] xlvi. 1-3, 5-6.   [2] xcviii. 7, 8.
[3] lxxxiv. 4, xciv. 9, xcviii. 10, xcix. 15, civ. 5; also "the great

and His Messiah: "And [1] he sat upon the throne of his glory, and the sum of the judgment was given unto him, unto the son of man; and he causes the sinners to be destroyed, and to perish from the face of the earth, and those also which have seduced the world: they shall be bound with chains, and imprisoned in their assembling place of destruction. And all evil shall vanish before him and depart: but the word of that son of man shall abide before the Lord of spirits." And so the tyrant kings, who, when it is too late, begin to profess repentance, are driven forth from the judge's presence, his sword not departing from their midst.[2]

As regards the future lot of the redeemed, the representations contained in the central part of the book appear as the most elevated. In the first part their condition is conceived rather as one of material blessing: it is a state of felicity upon earth; nature is generous with her gifts; not immortality, but long life, secured for the "elect," after the final judgment, by the fruit of the Tree of Life, and undisturbed by sorrow, or mourning, or pain, is the prospect held out by the seer to the faithful.[3] In the central part of

---

day of judgment," x. 6, xxii. 11, or "the great day," liv. 6. "The great judgment" is also mentioned xvi. 1, xix. 1, xxii. 4, xxv. 4, c. 4, ciii. 8.

[1] lxix. 27, 29.   [2] lxiii. 1, 11.

[3] xxiv. 3-5, xxv. 1-5. The source of such representations may be seen in Gen. ii. 9, iii. 22, Is. xxxv. 10, lxv. 19-23. With the "tree of life" comp. also 4 Ezra (Engl. 2 Ezra) viii. 52, Rev. ii. 7, xxii. 2 (Ezek. xlvii. 12), 14, 19.

GROWTH OF BELIEF IN A FUTURE STATE. 83

the book, the ideal is higher and more spiritual. Heaven is no longer separate from earth; they are merged, and form the home of one great community, with God and the Messiah in their midst: "And [1] here saw I another vision: the dwellings of the just, and the resting-places of the holy. . . . And I saw their dwellings under the wings of the Lord of spirits; and all the just and the elect before him are adorned with the light of fire, and their mouths are filled with praise, and their lips adore the name of the Lord of spirits, and righteousness ceaseth not before him." Again, "And [2] in that day will I cause my Chosen One (the Messiah) to dwell among them, and I will change the heaven and make it a blessing and a light for ever, and I will change the earth and make it a blessing, and cause mine elect to dwell upon it; but they that commit sin and wrong shall not tread therein." "And [3] the Lord of spirits will dwell over them; and they shall dwell together with that son of man, and shall eat, and lie down, and rise up with him to all eternity." "And [4] the just shall be in the light of the sun, and the elect in the light of eternal life; and there shall be no end to the days of their life, and the days of the holy shall be without number." The phrase "eternal life" [5] may be borrowed from Dan. xii. 2: the "age (*or* world) to come," [6]

[1] xxxix. 4, 7.   [2] xlv. 4, 5.   [3] lxii. 14.   [4] lviii. 3.
[5] Also xxxvii. 4, xl. 9.
[6] The common post-Biblical Jewish expression for the future state (הָעוֹלָם הַבָּא, or, in Aramaic, עָלְמָא דְאָתֵי): so for instance in the Mishnah, frequently. See also below, pp. 91, 92, 98.

occurs for the first time in the passage I am about to quote, addressed to Enoch in another vision. "He[1] calls *Peace* to thee in the name of the age to come; for thence proceeds peace since the creation of the world; and thus will it be unto thee into eternity, and from eternity unto eternity. And all who in future walk in thy path (thou whom righteousness forsaketh not for ever), their dwelling-places will be with thee, and they will not be separated from thee in eternity, and from eternity to eternity."

On the other hand, the punishment allotted to the wicked after judgment is thus described:—"Henceforth[2] know ye that all your violence which ye do is written down every day until the day of your judgment." "Woe[3] to you, sinners, when ye vex the righteous, on the day of sharp pain, and burn them with fire; it shall be recompensed to you according to your works. Woe to you, ye perverse of heart, ye that are vigilant to devise evil: fear shall come upon you, and there shall be none to save you. Woe to you, ye sinners, for on account of the words of your mouth, and the works of your hands, which ye have done in godlessness, ye shall burn in a lake of fiery flames." And elsewhere, the punishment of the wicked is described as a killing of their souls—a phrase which does not, however, imply annihilation: "Their[4] names shall be blotted out of the books of the holy, and their seed shall perish for ever; and

---

[1] lxxi. 15-16.   [2] xcviii. 8.   [3] c. 7-9.
[4] cviii. 3: cf. xxii. 13, xcix. 11; also liii. 5, lxii. 2, lxiii. 9, 11.

GROWTH OF BELIEF IN A FUTURE STATE. 85

their souls shall be killed: and they shall cry aloud and lament in a desolate waste, and shall burn in fire."
Time will not permit me to dwell upon the teaching of other writings belonging to the same period. Their examination, however, would not add any substantial feature to the picture already obtained from the Book of Enoch. Most of them, indeed, are far less explicit. It must suffice, then, to remark that while the Book of Jesus, the son of Sirach, occupies still the same standpoint as the Old Testament generally,[1] and regards death as the limit of all existence worthy of the name of "life," the philosophic author of the Book of Wisdom teaches expressly the immortality of the soul, and a future state of reward and punishment,[2] and that the so-called Psalms of Solomon,[3] written in Palestine when the Jews were smarting under the humiliation which they suffered at the hands of Pompey, affirm distinctly a resurrection: "The destruction of the sinner is for ever. . . . But they that fear the Lord shall rise again unto eternal life: and their life shall be in the light of the Lord, and it shall fail no more."[4]

The Jewish Targums, to which I now proceed, are

[1] Cf. Ecclus. xiv. 16, xvii. 27 f. (see p. 73, Note 6), xxii. 11, xlvi. 19 (comp. Jer. li. 39, 57), 20 (comp. 1 Sam. xxviii. 15 ff.), xlviii. 5. In xlviii. 11 the text and sense are both uncertain.
[2] ii. 23, iii. 1-4 ("The souls of the righteous are in the hand of God," &c.), vi. 18, 20, viii. 17, xv. 3.
[3] See Ryle and James, *Psalms of the Pharisees, commonly called the Psalms of Solomon* (1891).
[4] iii. 13-16; cf. xiii. 9-10, xiv. 2, 6, 7, xv. 13-15. Comp. Ryle and James, p. li, lii.

Aramaic versions of the Old Testament, made for the use of the Jews when Hebrew had ceased to be in general use as a spoken language. They were not, indeed, committed to writing until some time subsequently to the Christian era; but they embody interpretations which, no doubt, originated in many cases at a much earlier period. Their style varies. In historical narrative, it is, as a rule, literal. In the Prophets and Psalms, it is commonly (though not uniformly) more or less paraphrastic, sometimes, indeed, even to the perversion of the sense. Still, even when it is paraphrastic, if the Targum be read as an application or adaptation of the text, rather than as a strict interpretation of it, it will often be found to contain a just and suggestive thought. In the passages which I shall quote, it will be impossible to consider in each instance how far the interpretation is a just one or not; it must suffice to premise generally that in most cases the reference to a future life does not apparently lie within the scope of the text. It may be observed that the conceptions which in the Book of Enoch appear in the process of formation, and not always free from indistinctness, appear in the Targums as more complete, and clearly defined. It should be added, that there are grounds for regarding the Targums on the Hagiographa as later than those of either Onkelos on the Pentateuch, or of Jonathan on the Prophets.[1]

[1] The last two probably assumed their present form in the third or fourth century A.D.

The resurrection is mentioned—Hos. vi. 2: "He will quicken us for the days of consolation which are to come: in the day when the dead are quickened he will raise us up, and we shall live before him." xiv. 7 (Heb. 8): "They shall be gathered from among their captivities; they shall dwell under the shadow of their Messiah: the dead shall live, and prosperity shall be multiplied in the land." Isaiah xxvi. 19 (the passage already quoted as actually containing the idea) is thus paraphrased: "Thou art he that quickeneth the dead; the bones of their corpses thou raisest up; all that are cast down in the dust shall live to praise thee: for thy dew is a dew of light to them that observe the law; but the wicked, unto whom thou hast given might, but who have transgressed thy word, thou shalt deliver to Gehenna." xlii. 11: "Let the wilderness utter praise, the villages that inhabit the wilderness of the Arabians; let the dead utter praise, when they come forth from their long homes, from the tops of the rocks let them lift up their voice." xlv. 8: "Let the heavens do service above, and the clouds pour forth abundance: let the earth open, and the dead live, and righteousness be revealed together." And from the Targum on Zech. xiv. 4: "At that time the Lord shall take in his hand a great trumpet, and shall blow with it ten blasts to revive the dead: and he shall be revealed at that time in his might on the Mount of Olives, which is before Jerusalem, on the East, and the Mount of Olives shall be cleft in the midst thereof toward the

East and toward the West." The sequel may be stated in the words of a later Targum, on Cant. viii. 5 : "When the dead shall live, the Mount of Olives shall be divided, and all the dead of Israel shall come forth from beneath it."

The future judgment is alluded to (though not often explicitly) by the same title as in the Book of Enoch, the "great judgment" or the "great day." Ps. l. 3 : "The righteous wilt say in the day of the great judgment, Our God shall come and not keep silence." Josh. vii. 25 :[1] "The Lord trouble thee this day; but in the day of the great judgment thou shalt escape and be acquitted." 2 Sam. xxiii. 7 : "Their punishment is not by the hand of man, but they will be burnt with fire: they will be burnt when the tribunal of the great judgment shall be revealed, to sit upon the throne of judgment, to judge the world."

The second death (as in Rev. ii. 11, xx. 6, 14, xxi. 8), corresponding to the death of the soul in Enoch, is named, Deut. xxxiii. 6: "Let Reuben live in the life of eternity, and not die the second death." Is. lxv. 15 : "And ye shall leave your name for a curse unto my chosen, and the Lord shall kill you with the second death." Jer. li. 39, 57, where the prophet promises that Israel's foes shall sleep a perpetual sleep, and not awake: "And they shall die the second death, and not live for the age to come."[2]

---

[1] In the fragment of a "Jerusalem" Targum, cited on the margin of the Reuchlin Codex, and published by Lagarde, *Prophetae Chaldaice* (1872), p. vi, lines 28-29.

[2] Add Is. xxii. 14 Targ.: "Surely this iniquity shall not be

GROWTH OF BELIEF IN A FUTURE STATE. 89

Mention is made not unfrequently of Gehenna, and sometimes the opposite lots of the righteous and wicked are contrasted. Hosea xiv. 9 (Heb. 10): "The righteous, who walk" in the ways of God, "shall live in them in eternal life; but the wicked who walk not in them shall be delivered to Gehenna."[1] Nahum i. 8 *end:* "And his enemies he will deliver to Gehenna."[2] Ps. xlix. 9 (Heb. 10): "That he should live again unto eternal life, and not behold the judgment of Gehenna." Ps. cxl. 10: "Let hot burning coals alight upon them from heaven; let him cast them into the fire of Gehenna with glowing sparks, that they rise not again unto eternal life."[3] Is. xxxiii. 17: "The glory of the Shekhinah of the eternal King in his majesty shall thine eyes behold; thou shalt see and behold them that go down to the land of Gehenna," where the Hebrew says simply, "They shall see a land of distances" (*i.e.* a far-stretching land). Isa. lvii. 20: "But the wicked shall be tossed about in Gehenna, like the troubled sea,

---

forgiven you, until ye die the second death"; Is. lxv. 6 Targ.: "Behold it is written before me: I will not give you a respite in life, but I will render to you the vengeance of your sins, and I will deliver your bodies to the second death." See also Ps. xlix. 10 (Heb. 11) in the Antwerp Polyglott of 1569: "For he will see the wise ones of wickedness that they die the second death, and are judged in Gehenna."

[1] Hebrew text: "The just shall walk in them; but transgressors shall fall therein."

[2] Hebrew text: "Will pursue his enemies into darkness" (of the people of Nineveh).

[3] See Note H (p. 97).

which seeketh to be at rest, but is not able." And in the last verse of Isaiah, where, by a Rabbinical device, of which other examples might be quoted,[1] the Hebrew word rendered "abhorring" is divided into two, which are interpreted to mean "sufficiency of seeing": "And they shall go forth, and look upon the carcases of the guilty men who have rebelled against my word, because their souls shall not die, and their fire shall not be quenched; but the wicked shall be judged in Gehenna, until the righteous shall say concerning them, We have seen enough."

Paradise, or, to use the Aramaic expression,[2] the "Garden of Eden," is but seldom named in the Targums. It will be sufficient to cite two passages, one from a Targum[3] (not the ordinary one) on Isa. xlv. 7 ("I form the light and create darkness"): "I ordain the light of life eternal for the righteous in the Garden of Eden, and create the darkness of Gehenna for the wicked"; the other from that on the Song of Songs, where the "gar en enclosed" (Cant. iv. 12) is interpreted of the "Garden of Eden, into which no one hath authority to enter save the righteous, whose souls are conveyed thither by the hand of angels." More commonly the Targumists are content to give expression to their belief in a life of future blessedness, by the introduction, where the context was suitable, of the phrase "in the

---

[1] See Note I (p. 97).
[2] See Note J (p. 93).
[3] From the same margin of the Reuchlin Codex mentioned above: Lagarde, *l. c.* p. xxxi, lines 22-23.

age (*or* world) to come," or "eternal life," sometimes contrasting with it "this age (*or* world)." Thus Lev. xviii. 5 : "And ye shall keep my statutes and my judgments, which if a man do, he shall live in the life eternal." 1 Sam. xxv. 29 : " Let the soul of my lord be hidden in the treasury of eternal life before the Lord thy God." Isa. iv. 3 : "And it shall be that he that is left shall return to Zion, and he that observeth the law shall be established in Jerusalem ; he shall be called holy ; every one that is written down for life eternal shall see the consolation of Jerusalem." Isa. lviii. 11 : " And the Lord shall guide thee continually, and shall satisfy thy soul in years of drought, and quicken thy body in life eternal."[1] More frequently in the later Targums, as in that on the Psalms : for instance, Ps. xviii. 28 (Heb. 29) : " The Lord my God will bring me forth from darkness into light, he will let me look upon the consolation of the age that is to come for the righteous." Ps. xxx. 5 (Heb. 6) : Because his wrath is for a moment ; life eternal is his favour." Ps. xxxix. 5 (Heb. 6) : " But all are counted as nought ; but all the righteous endure to life eternal."[2] Ps. lxiii. 3 (Heb. 4) : "For better is thy mercy which thou wilt show to the righteous in the age to come, than the life that thou hast given to

[1] Cf. 2 Sam. vii. 19, where "for a great while to come " (lit. *afar off*) is represented in the Targ. by "for the world to come."

[2] The Hebrew words of the text being taken as if they could mean " (They are) all vanity ; every man standeth firm," and then being further paraphrased.

the wicked in this age."[1] Ps. xcii. 10: "Lo thine enemies, O Lord, lo thine enemies shall perish in the world to come." Ps. cxxxix. 18: "If I should count them in this world, they are more in number than the sand; when I awake in the world to come, I am still with thee."

Sometimes, lastly, a possible misconception is guarded against by the limitation of the text to the present world. Thus, Isa. v. 20: "Woe unto those that say to the wicked who prosper in this world, Ye are good." Ps. lxxiii. 12: "Lo, such are the wicked who dwell at ease in this world; they obtain riches and acquire substance." Eccl. vi. 8: "What advantage hath the wise in this world more than the fool?" But in the Targum to this book, the contrast between the two worlds is throughout made exceptionally prominent, as though with the object of guarding against sceptical inferences which might otherwise appear capable of being deduced from the text.[2]

That the Jews, meditating upon the writings of the Old Testament, should thus have arrived at the clearly-defined hope of a future life, cannot form occasion for surprise. For, indeed, the immortality of the human soul, its eternal relation to the Creator

---

[1] Cf. *v.* 4 (Heb. 5): "So will I bless thee while I live in this world: in the name of thy Word will I spread out my hands in prayer in the world to come"; lxvi. 9: "Who placed our souls in the life of the world to come"; also xvii. 14: "But the righteous who deliver their souls for thy sake unto death upon earth, their portion is in life eternal."

[2] See Note K (p. 98).

GROWTH OF BELIEF IN A FUTURE STATE. 93

who has called it into being, is presupposed in the Old Testament revelation; and there are passages in which the idea is on the verge of expression, or, as our Lord showed on a celebrated occasion, latent, even though it be only enunciated explicitly in the later writings of the Old Testament canon. The intimations of a future life, more or less distinct, thus contained in the Old Testament, were developed, on the basis of prophetic representations of the future triumph of the kingdom of God, in the manner which I have sought to-day to indicate. These developments were such that, in certain cases, and interpreted probably in a more spiritual sense than belonged to their original intention, they could be accepted and appropriated by the first teachers of the Christian faith. In its eschatology, as in its Christology, the Book of Enoch is based essentially upon the Old Testament; it is an imaginative development and elaboration of elements derived thence. Of distinctively Christian truth, of the truths, that is, which centre in, or radiate from, the doctrine of the Incarnation, it does not exhibit a trace. Its resemblance to the writings of the New Testament is limited to externals. The utmost that can be said of it, in this respect, is that it may have lent to the Apostles, perhaps even to our Lord, certain figures and expressions in which they could suitably and conveniently clothe their ideas. But this is no more than what happened in numberless other instances, in which the teaching of both Christ and His disciples is cast in the mould of contemporary Jewish thought. Even where the resemblance appears to be the closest, a careful comparison will disclose significant features of difference. The originality of the fundamental conceptions of Christianity is not impaired by the acknowledgment that Jewish thought, reflecting upon the Old Testament, may have provided symbols for their expression, or, in the case of less distinctive ideas, may have even reached them in anticipation. It remains that, in its full significance, the doctrine of a future life was first enunciated in the Gospel; and that it was He who "abolished death," who also was the first to bring "life and incorruption to light."

ADDITIONAL NOTES TO SERMON IV.

NOTE A.

See Job x. 20—21 (Ps. xxxix. 13), 22, xiv. 21, Eccl. ix. 5, 10. "Sheol," in general conception, corresponds to the Greek Hades, and must be carefully distinguished from "the grave." The distinction is rightly preserved in the Revised Version. It is true, there are particular phrases, as "to go down to Sheol," the general sense of which is sufficiently represented by the English idiomatic expression "to go down to the grave"; and this has accordingly been retained in the Revised Version : but "Sheol" in such cases stands on the margin (*e. g.* 1 Sam. ii. 6, Is. xxxviii. 10), and elsewhere it is used in the text. Occasionally "hell" has been retained from the Authorised Version (Is. v. 14, xiv. 9, 15) : this, it need scarcely be said, is used (as in the Creed) in the old sense of the term, and not in that of a place of torment. The ordinary Hebrew belief was conscious of no distinction in the future lot of the righteous and the wicked. The impossibility of a return, or resurrection, from Sheol was also strongly felt (Job vii. 9 f., xiv. 7-12, Jer. li. 39, 57, Is. xxvii. 14) : the possibility of another life entrances Job (Job xiv. 14 f., R.V.), but he rejects it as incredible (*vv.* 16-22). Comp. A. F. Kirkpatrick, *The Psalms (Book I.*), in the *Cambridge Bible for Schools*, pp. lxxv-lxxvii ; and see also the Essay on "Jewish and Heathen conceptions of a Future State" in the late Dr. Mozley's *Lectures and other Theological Papers* (1883), p. 26 ff.

NOTE B.

Is. lxv. 22. The view of the prophet is that in the future which he here depicts, the ordinary occupations of life will still be pursued (*v.* 21), but there will be a cessation of the drawbacks and disappointments by which they are commonly accompanied (*vv.* 20, 22ᵃ, 23), and the power of death will be limited (*v.* 22ᵇ) : cf. *v.* 20 (death at the age of 100 years will be counted premature). In xxv. 8 the power of death is represented as abolished altogether.

NOTE C.

The word here rendered "Shades" is *rephaim* (lit., as it seems, *relaxed, weak ones*), which occurs besides in *v.* 14, Job xxvi. 5, Ps. lxxxviii. 10 (Heb. 11), Prov. ii. 18, ix. 18, xxi. 16. The same term was in use among the Phoenicians ; thus, in the sepulchral inscription of Tabnith (*c.* 300 B.C.), found near Sidon, there is a prayer that any one who disturbs the tomb may find no "resting-place with the Shades" (see the writer's *Notes on the Hebrew text of Samuel*, 1890, pp. xxvii, xxix).

NOTE D.

The word rendered "contempt" (R.V. *marg.* "abhorrence") is a peculiar one, and is in all probability borrowed from Is. lxvi. 24 (the only other passage in which it occurs), where it is applied to the putrefying carcases of the "transgressors"— *i.e.* in particular, the disbelieving, renegade Israelites (see xlvi. 8, lxv. 2-5, 11, lxvi. 5, 17)—whom the prophet represents as destroyed by a sudden Divine intervention (lxvi. 17-19), and whose dead bodies, exposed in one of the valleys near Jerusalem, will be a continual spectacle of horror to the pilgrims visiting the Holy City (*vv.* 23, 24).

NOTE E.

Eccl. iii. 17, xi. 9, xii. 14. But the interpretation of these passages is doubtful ; and in view of the uncertainty expressed generally in the book with respect to a future life (see especially iii. 19-21, R.V., where the doctrine is treated avowedly as unproven), it is more probable that the reference is to temporal judgments. Comp. the writer's *Introduction*, p. 448. Dr. Mozley, *l. c.* p. 51, has been misled by the Authorised Version of Eccl. iii. 21, the punctuation which this implies giving rise to an unidiomatic and, indeed, an impossible Hebrew sentence, while that expressed by the R.V. is natural and regular.

NOTE F.

It should however be noted that in the Book of Daniel the period immediately following the death of Antiochus Epiphanes, and end of his persecutions (Dan. xi. 31-45), which is marked by the resurrection of Israelites (xii. 1, 2), appears to be identical with that to which the advent of the Messiah, and triumph of the saints, are assigned (vii. 11-14, 18-27).

NOTE G.

On the characteristics of "Apocalyptic Literature," comp. J. Drummond, *The Jewish Messiah* (1877), pp. 1-132; J. E. H. Thomson, *Books which influenced our Lord and His Apostles* (1891), p. 193 ff.; and the references in the writer's *Introduction*, p. 482.

NOTE H.

See also the Targ. on Ps. xxi. 9 (Heb. 10): "Jehovah shall devour them in his anger, and the burning of Gehenna will consume them"; xxxvii. 20 (on "they consume in smoke, they consume away"): "The wicked shall come to an end, and be consumed in the smoke of Gehenna"; xlix. 10 (Heb. 11): "For the wise will see the wicked judged in Gehenna"; 14 (Heb. 15): "Their bodies shall waste away in Gehenna"; 15 (Heb. 16): "But God will save my soul from the judgment of Gehenna"; lv. 23 (Heb. 24) (for "the pit of depression"); lxix. 15 (Heb. 16) (for "the pit"); lxxxiv. 6 (Heb. 7): "The wicked who pass over to the depths of Gehenna, weeping with weepings, make it like a spring"; lxxxviii. 12 (Heb. 13) ("the darkness of Gehenna"); ciii. 4 (for "the pit"); cxx. 4 ("with coals of broom, kindled in Gehenna beneath"), &c.

NOTE I.

See the writer's *Notes on the Hebrew text of Samuel*, p lxxxiv, or (from Aquila, who followed Rabbinical principles of exegesis) the Preface to Field's *Hexapla*, p. xxii f. Jerome, who was guided sometimes by Jewish teachers and translators, has the same interpretation of the Hebrew word in Is. lxvi. 24, " et erunt *usque ad satietatem visionis* omni carni "

98 ADDITIONAL NOTES TO SERMON IV.

(*i. e.* דִּרְאוֹן read as דִּי רָאוֹן). "Scape-goat" is an example of a rendering based ultimately upon a similar exegetical device, which has preserved its place in the Authorised Version to the present day (עֲזָאזֵל "Azazel," read as עֵז אָזֵל, *i. e.* "the departing goat," Symmachus τράγος ἀπερχόμενος, Aquila τράγος ἀπολυόμενος, Jerome *caper emissarius*).

NOTE J.

The *word* "paradise" (which is of Persian origin), though it is found in the Targums, is never used there in the sense which it has acquired in Christian literature from Luke xxiii. 43, but only in the general sense (which it has also in Hebrew, Cant. iv. 3, Neh. ii. 8, Eccl. ii. 5) of *orchard* or *park*.

NOTE K.

Thus on Eccl. i. 3 ("What profit hath man of all his labour wherein he laboureth under the sun?") the Targum has: What profit hath a man after he dies of all his labour wherein he laboureth under the sun in this world, except he occupy himself in the law, that he may receive a perfect reward unto the world to come before the Lord of the world? i. 9, And there is no new thing in this world under the sun. iii. 22, And I saw that there is nothing better in this world than that a man should rejoice in his good works, and eat, and drink, and gladden his heart; for that is his good portion in this world to purchase with it the world to come. vii. 15, There is a just man that perisheth in his righteousness in this world, but his justice (*or* merit) is preserved for him for the world to come; and there is a wicked man that prolongeth his days in his sins, and the reckoning of his evil deeds is reserved for him for the world to come, that vengeance may be taken of him in the day of the great judgment. And frequently besides. The expression "that world" (Luke xx. 35) is also used of the age to come in the same Targum (on v. 15, vi. 4, 9, vii. 14, viii. 15, x. 19).

SERMON V.[1]

THE HEBREW PROPHETS.

Amos ii. 11-12 : "And I raised up of your sons for prophets, and of your young men for Nazirites. Is it not even thus, O ye children of Israel? saith the LORD. But ye gave the Nazirites wine to drink; and commanded the prophets, saying, Prophesy not."

THE Book of Amos, brief though it is, offers much to engage the reader's attention. With the doubtful exception of Joel, Amos is the earliest of the prophets whose writings are incorporated in the Old Testament canon. Himself a native of Judah, he receives a commission to preach in the Northern Kingdom ; and appears at the royal sanctuary of Bethel, towards the end of the long reign of Jeroboam II.,[2] about 750 years before Christ. In the case of the earlier prophets, owing to the habit of the Hebrew historians to re-cast and amplify, in the sense of their own times, the sayings transmitted to them from an earlier age, it is often difficult to feel assured that the prophecies reported in the historical books are before us in their original colouring and dress ; in the case of Amos,

[1] Preached at St. Mary's, before the University, on Sunday, Oct. 16, 1887.
[2] B.C. c. 786—746. Compare the table in the writer's *Isaiah*, p. 13.

we have the witness of a contemporary, a keen and acute observer, furnishing us himself with a picture of the beliefs and institutions of his day, describing to us, directly or by allusion, the condition of life and society in Northern Israel, declaring, freely and unrestrainedly, the impression which they produced upon him, and the motives impelling him to pass judgment upon them. In the text, he alludes to two classes of God-directed men, one the Nazirites, men who by a life of abstinence protested against the sensuality and indulgence prevalent about them, and who, from the nature of the allusion, must have formed a conspicuous element in society; the other, the prophets. It is as giving us a personal record of the work, and aims, and convictions of a prophet at this early date, that the Book of Amos acquires peculiar interest. Thus the authority which a prophet of that day claimed is expressed by him in the memorable words:—" Surely the Lord Jehovah will do nothing, but he revealeth his secret to his servants the prophets. The lion hath roared, who will not fear? The Lord Jehovah hath spoken, who can but prophesy?"[1] The prophet came forward as the spokesman and representative of his God; and the impulse prompting him to deliver the message which he had received was an irresistible one. Hosea, the younger contemporary of Amos, speaks of the prophet in similar terms. Thus alluding both to the prominent position which they took, and to their authority,

[1] Amos iii. 7, 8.

he writes :—"I have also spoken unto the prophets, and I have multiplied visions; and by the hand of the prophets have I used similitudes."[1] And just as Amos in the text implies that their preaching was apt to be unpalatable to the people, so Hosea alludes to the resentment which his own observation had shown him that it provoked: "As for the prophet, a fowler's snare is in all his ways, and enmity in the house of his God."[2]

The history of Israel, it has been said, is a history of prophecy. It is a history in which men of prophetic rank and name stand at the great turning-points of the people's life and direct the movements. It is a history, further, in which the inner progress of the nation was largely determined by the prophets, who sustained or intensified the religious life of the community, and stood superior to their contemporaries, as the exponents and representatives of ethical and theological truth. I propose this morning to offer a few illustrations of their work in the two spheres of politics and morals. The insight and independence possessed by the prophets fitted them, in a singular degree, to be the political advisers of their nation. They were in closer sympathy than most of their fellow-countrymen with the needs of the time; they apprehended more quickly and accurately what the situation of the nation demanded; they saw beyond the seeming interests of the moment, and were regardless either of popular favour, or of

[1] Hos. xii. 10.   [2] Hos. ix. 8.

interests of party. Surveying the nations around, the prophets descry in advance the tendencies and impulses hidden from ordinary eyes, and lay down the principles by which, as the course of history shapes itself, the welfare of their own nation demands that it should be guided. They denounce the popular statesmanship of the day, and expose the fallacies which underlie it. They attack the national sins and shortcomings, showing how they must inevitably work out their natural results, in a deterioration of national character and a growing inability to meet danger calmly. Amos sees society in the Northern Kingdom, in spite of the brilliancy and long prosperity of Jeroboam's reign, morally vitiated and corrupt. The nobles of Samaria, so far from evincing anxiety for the public weal, " put far the evil day," and are abandoned to self-indulgence and luxury;[1] the heathen themselves are invited to testify to the violence and disorder prevalent in the capital;[2] and each section of his prophecy ends with a dark vision of approaching disaster and misfortune.[3] In the plaintive, halting rhythm of the Hebrew elegiac,[4] he sings:—

The virgin of Israel is fallen; she shall no more rise:
She lieth forsaken upon her land; there is none to raise her up.

He speaks again, even more significantly and directly: "Behold, I raise up against you, O house of Israel, saith Jehovah, the God of hosts, a nation;

---

[1] Amos vi. 3-6.   [2] Amos iii. 9.
[3] Amos ii. 14-16; iii. 14 f.; v. 26 (R.V. *marg.*), 27; vi. 14; vii. 17, &c.
[4] See the writer's *Introduction*, p. 429 f.   [5] Amos v. 2.

and they shall afflict you from the entering in of Hamath unto the brook of the Arabah."[1] The limits here indicated are exactly those to which, according to the history, the then reigning monarch had just successfully restored the dominion of Israel.[2] The words of Amos were soon to be verified. Within sixteen years the inhabitants of the north-eastern districts were deported by Tiglath-Pileser to Assyria:[3] within thirty years the Northern Kingdom had ceased to exist.[4] The prophet had interpreted but too truly the signs of the times. He had seen in advance the formidable influence which Assyria was destined soon to exercise upon the fortunes of Palestine: he perceived how little fitted the political leaders of Samaria were to guide their state safely through the approaching crisis; he set before them the course which there was hope might at least partially, if it was not too late, avert the ruin;[5] but he saw, not the less clearly, what the final issue would be.

Other illustrations of the same faculty possessed by the prophets are not far to seek. The prophets who were popular with the people were those who, while finding nothing in their conduct to censure, held out to them visions of felicity and peace, to be realized in the immediate future, without any such antecedent period of discipline or probation as is always postulated by the canonical prophets. Such prophets are

---

[1] Amos vi. 14.   [2] See 2 Kings xiv. 25.   [3] B.C. 734.
[4] The capture of Samaria followed almost immediately after the accession of Sargon, B.C. 722.   [5] Amos v. 15.

often alluded to, for instance, by Micah, Isaiah, and Jeremiah : they are described as merely echoing the superficial sentiment of the masses, or as being " prophets of their own hearts."[1] In Jeremiah's time, when the invader was at the door, they persistently promised peace ;[2] and after the Chaldæans had carried away the vessels of the Temple to Babylon, they promised their restoration, and the return of the exiled King, Jehoiachin, " within two years."[3] Jeremiah's eye had seen more truly. Not only had he foreseen the ruin which the policy of the last kings of Judah was accelerating ; he foresaw besides, in its true magnitude, the dimensions which the empire of Nebuchadnezzar was destined to attain. With an unfaltering hand, in bold and clear strokes, he constructs the future. No sooner had Nebuchadnezzar, in 604 B.C., gained his crucial victory over Pharaoh-Necho at Carchemish, than the prophet grasps the idea that the empire of the then known world is to be his : he greets the conqueror with the ode of triumph, preserved in chapter xlvi., promising him further successes ; he styles him " Jehovah's servant,"[4] and declares that the safety of Judah is to be found in submission to his sway.[5] For seventy years the Chaldæan supremacy should be maintained. At the

---

[1] Mic. ii. 11, iii. 5, 11 ; Is. xxx. 10 ; Jer. v. 12, 13, xxiii. 16, 26 ; Ezek. xiii. 2, 10.

[2] Jer. vi. 14, xiv. 13-15, xxiii. 16 f.   [3] Jer. xxviii. 3 f.

[4] Jer. xxv. 9 : so some eight years afterwards, xxvii. 6 ; and again after the fall of Jerusalem, xliii. 10.

[5] Jer. xxv. 8-11, xxvii. 12-14.

end of that period, the exiled Jews should be visited and restored to their place.[1] The prophets, as is natural, accommodate their views to the changing movements which sway the political world. A century before, Isaiah had promised that the tide of Assyrian aggression should be rolled back from the rock of Zion, and leave the Jewish state, not indeed untouched by the fury of the waves, but still standing and secure. Now, Jeremiah saw that the hand of Nebuchadnezzar was destined to prevail, and taught that the safety of the city lay in its acceptance of the inevitable. He was persecuted by political opponents, he was charged with lack of patriotism and courage, but the issue showed that he had seen aright. Fifty or sixty years afterwards another crucial moment arrived in the history of the chosen people. Was Judah to lose its individuality in the land of its exile, to be gradually assimilated, like its brethren of the ten tribes, to the nations among whom it dwelt? Or was it to return to its ancient home, and complete the destined course of its history? There were many who had followed the advice given by Jeremiah to the first exiles;[2] they had settled down and found their ease in their adopted home. They were content to remain where they were; they had no high aspirations for the future; the magnificence of Babylonian idolatry overawed them; the strength and resources of the proud imperial city were able, they felt assured, to repel every assailant.[3] There was a prophet who saw otherwise

[1] Jer. xxix. 10.   [2] Jer. xxix. 5-7.
[3] See the expressions of despair, which the prophet proceeds

—the author of the great series of discourses, which now form the last twenty-seven chapters of the Book of Isaiah. Did they deem it impossible that the power of the Chaldæans could be shaken? The prophet meets their doubts in the profound and pregnant words: "All flesh is grass, and all the goodliness thereof is as the flower of the field. . . . The grass withereth, the flower fadeth; but the word of our God shall stand for ever."[1] Did they point to the pomp and splendour of the Babylonian idols? He aims against them the keen shafts of irony and satire.[2] Cyrus is Jehovah's appointed agent, and though his triumphal progress may throw the nations of Asia into consternation and drive them in terror to their idol-gods,[3] Israel has no ground for fear: a noble and august future is still before it.[4] Did they, still unconvinced, allege that the facts refuted the prophet's too sanguine view? He replies: "For my thoughts are not as your thoughts, neither are your ways my ways, saith Jehovah:" your estimate of the facts is a false one; the word spoken cannot be recalled; and the joy with which, ere long, you will leave Babylon behind you, will be your involuntary attestation of its truth.[5]

---

to controvert, in Is. xl. 27, xlix. 14, 24 (to be read with the second part of the margin of the Revised Version); also xliv. 21 (*Israel* bidden to take to heart the folly of attaching any importance to the idols of Babylon, satirized in xliv. 10-20).

[1] Is. xl. 6-8.
[2] Is. xli. 5-7 (the nations of the earth manufacturing new idols, in the hope of arresting the progress of Cyrus); xliv. 9-20; xlvi. 1-2; cf. xlvii. 9-15.
[3] Is. xli. 2-7.   [4] Is. xli. 8-20.   [5] Is. lv. 8-12.

An attentive study of their writings shows that the prophets are primarily the teachers of their own generation. It is the political mistakes, the social abuses, the moral shortcomings, of their own age which they set themselves to correct. To be sure, they assert principles which are of universal validity, and capable, therefore, of application in new and altered circumstances; but the special forms which these principles assume in their hands show that they have been deliberately adopted to meet the needs of their own time. Prophecy subserved moral purposes: and its primary scope was the practical guidance, in life and thought, of those amongst whom the prophet lived. This fact affords us a criterion for estimating the temporal predictions of the prophets. The predictive element in the prophets is not so great as, perhaps, is sometimes supposed. Not only do the prophets deal with their actual present much more largely than is popularly imagined to be the case, but even in their announcements relative to the future, the amount of exact and minute prediction is less, probably, than might antecedently have been expected. The prophet's theme is developed with an artist's hand. He constructs a picture for the purpose of representing it in its completeness, and his genius supplies him with images of surprising beauty and force. But the imagery is merely the external dress in which the idea is clothed; and it is a vain and false literalism that would demand a place for its details in the fulfilment. There has been no highway such as Isaiah pictured for the return of

SERMON V.

the banished Israelites from Assyria:[1] no pillar, or obelisk, reminds the traveller entering Egypt, that the country is devoted to the worship of the true God:[2] Sennacherib perished by the sword in his own land; and the vast funeral pyre which the same prophet conceived as prepared for him, and which he saw in imagination already being kindled by Jehovah's breath,[3] is but the form under which he depicts the completeness of the Assyrians' ruin. So, again, Isaiah's sense of the weakness of Egyptian nationality, and its inability to resist any determined assailant, finds expression in a prophecy in which he expands this thought, and with a keen appreciation of national characteristics, applies it over the entire area of Egyptian civilization.[4] Their figures, therefore, as this example shows, though not to be understood too literally, are not idly chosen; they stand in a real relation to the thought to be expressed, and will be found, if properly studied, to be its suitable and adequate exponent. Other prophecies, again, relating to the future, are rather of the nature of solemn denunciation than prediction in the strict sense of the term; they indicate the issue to which a policy, or course of action, may naturally be expected to lead, without claiming to announce it categorically as a prediction. Other predictions, as is expressly taught by Jeremiah,[5] are nullified by a change supervening in the moral situation: uttered conditionally, and on the basis of a particular combination of

---

[1] Is. xi. 16.   [2] Is. xix. 19, 20.
[3] Is. xxx. 33.   [4] Is. xix. 1-17.   [5] Jer. xviii. 7-10.

circumstances, when the circumstances alter, the issue, it is evident, may change also, and the prediction be thus no longer applicable. And of others, sometimes remarkably definite, we do not know whether they were fulfilled or not, as for example, Isaiah's declaration of the humiliation of Moab within three years, or of Kedar within one year, or of the banishment of Shebna.[1]

But when the necessary deductions have been made upon grounds such as these, there remain undoubted and remarkable examples of true predictions; not, indeed, predictions relating to a remote future, without interest or significance for the prophet's own contemporaries, but predictions declaring the issue of a present political complication, or announcing beforehand a coming event, especially events having a bearing on the progress of the Kingdom of God. Instances of such prediction, verified within the limit of a few years, have been quoted already. Jeremiah's prophecy of the expiration of the Chaldæan supremacy after seventy years, is no exception to this rule; the restoration which then followed was but the termination of the same phase of history, of which Jeremiah's contemporaries in 604 were witnessing the commencement. Two or three other examples may be worth referring to. One of the boldest, and also one

[1] Is. xvi. 14; xxi. 16 f.; xxii. 18. Shebna is mentioned afterwards, in 701 B.C. (Is. xxxvi. 3; xxxvii. 2), as no longer holding the important office of Governor of the Palace (which is filled now, in accordance with Isaiah's promise, xxii. 20 f., by Eliakim); but he has not—at least prior to that year—been banished: he still retains a place, as "scribe," among the king's ministers.

of the clearest, is afforded by the Book of Isaiah. Isaiah, a year before the event, predicted, not the siege merely of Jerusalem by the Assyrian armies (which, in our ignorance of the precise circumstances, we are unable to affirm might not conceivably have been reached by political calculation), but the termination of the siege by a sudden and unexpected disaster dispersing the attacking forces. "Ah, Ariel, Ariel, the city where David encamped! add ye a year to the year, let the feasts run their round; then will I distress Ariel, and there shall be mourning and lamentation. And I will camp against thee round about, and will lay siege against thee with a fort, and I will raise siege works against thee. But the multitude of thy foes shall be like small dust, and the multitude of the terrible ones as the chaff that passeth away; and it shall be at an instant, suddenly."[1] So different did the prospect appear to the people of the city, that they could attach no meaning to the prophet's words, and stared at him as he spoke in blank astonishment and incredulity.[2] But Isaiah is confident, and does not shrink from repeating his assurances. The passage I have quoted is but the first of a series of utterances, in all of which he describes under varying imagery a sudden and mysterious disaster, which will annihilate Judah's foes. Thus shortly afterwards we read: "As birds flying, so will Jehovah of Hosts protect Jerusalem; he will protect and deliver it, he will pass over and preserve it. And the Assyrian shall fall with the sword, not of

[1] Is. xxix. 1-3, 5.   [2] Is. xxix. 9.

man; and the sword, not of man, shall devour him: and he shall flee from the sword, and his young men shall be set to task work."[1] And, a little later, probably while the troops of Sennacherib were massing close at hand in the Philistine territory: "The nations rush like the rushing of many waters, but he shall rebuke them, and they shall flee afar off, and shall be chased as the chaff of the mountains before the wind, and like the whirling dust before the storm. At eventide behold confusion: before the morning he is not!"[2] And, still later, when the last hope of escape seemed almost to have been cut off, and the fate of the city, to human eyes, must have appeared to be sealed: "At the noise of the tumult, the peoples are fled; at the lifting up of thyself the nations are scattered."[3] The vagueness or obscurity which sometimes appears to hang over the prophet's words, can often be removed, when it is possible to throw upon them the light of history. On a bas-relief now in the British Museum there is the representation of a warrior king seated upon his throne of state: around are seen chariots and armed attendants; in front there advances a train of crouching captives; an inscription above exhibits the words, "Sennacherib, king of multitudes, king of Assyria, seated on a lofty throne, receives the spoil of the city of Lachish."[4] A

[1] Is. xxxi. 5, 8.   [2] Is. xvii. 13-14.   [3] Is. xxx. iii. 3.
[4] See Schrader, *Cuneiform Inscriptions and the Old Testament*, p. 287 (Engl. Tr., i. p. 280). Photographs of this interesting bas-relief are published by Messrs. Mansell, 2 Percy Street, Rathbone Place, London (Nos. 433, 434, 436 of the Assyrian series).

voice has risen out of the ruins of Kouyunjik to interpret the Hebrew prophet to this generation. Isaiah continues, apostrophizing the enemy: "And your spoil shall be gathered as the caterpillar gathereth; as locusts leap, shall they leap upon it."[1] The varying imagery which the prophet employs warns us that we must, as before, be on our guard against undue literalism in interpretation; but the fundamental thought which throughout underlies it, is in entire agreement with the event; and whether it was a pestilence, or some other agency, that caused the destruction of the Assyrian host, its occurrence at the time required for the salvation of the city, was a coincidence beyond the reach of human prevision or calculation. Other instances, if not so brilliant, yet not less convincing, might readily be found. Damascus capitulated to Tiglath-Pileser, literally within the limits of time anticipated by Isaiah,[2] and the fall of Samaria was not postponed many years beyond it. It would have been particularly interesting to notice Jeremiah's announcement of the spot in Tahpanhes on which Nebuchadnezzar, upon entering Egypt, should erect his royal throne.[3] Until recently, no independent evidence of an invasion of Egypt by Nebuchadnezzar, was known to exist; but two inscriptions lately discovered now attest it,[4] and cylinders

---

[1] Is. xxxiii. 4. See more fully, on the passages referred to, the writer's volume on Isaiah, in the "Men of the Bible" series, chap. vii. p. 66 ff.
[2] Is. viii. 4.   [3] Jer. xliii. 10.
[4] See Wiedemann, *Aegyptische Zeitschrift*, 1878, pp. 2-6, 87-89,

inscribed with his name have been disinterred almost upon the very site indicated by Jeremiah.[1] An impartial criticism, while, on the one hand, owning that temporal predictions exist which have been apparently unfulfilled, and admitting the probability that in the case of such as refer to a distant future, they have been incorrectly dated, or not transmitted to us in their original form, will, on the other hand, frankly acknowledge such as are beyond reasonable doubt or suspicion, and will not seek to eliminate them, or minimize their significance, by special pleading.

Ethically, the prophets play the *rôle* of what we should term social reformers. They attack the abuses always conspicuous in an Eastern aristocracy; they assert with uncompromising persistency the claims of honesty, justice, philanthropy, and mercy. Certainly, the most ancient Hebrew legislation known to us, the Decalogue and Book of the Covenant,[2] had placed such claims in the forefront; and the prophets do not, in this respect, so much advance theoretically as apply old principles to new situations, and re-assert them with fresh emphasis and energy. To purify justice, to reform religion, to fight against inconsistency, to redress social wrongs, are the aims common to all the prophets. Amos, introducing the main

Gesch. Aegyptens von Psammetich I. bis auf Alexander den Grossen, 1880, p. 167-169; Schrader, *Cuneiform Inscriptions and the O. T.*, on 2 Kings xxiv. 1 (p. 363 f.).

[1] See the *Academy*, 1884, vol. xxv., p. 51.
[2] Ex. xx.-xxiii.

theme of his prophecy, shows both originality and breadth of view. Casting his eye upon the nations around, Damascus, Gaza, Tyre, Edom, Ammon, Moab, he fastens upon some act of cruelty or inhumanity of which each has been guilty, and declares the judgment impending upon it.[1] Israel might listen thus far with equanimity : but the prophet ends by applying to the privileged nation the same standard :— "Thus saith Jehovah : For three transgressions of Israel, and for four, I will not turn away the punishment thereof, because they sold the righteous for silver, and the poor for the sake of a pair of shoes ; that pant after the dust of the earth on the head of the poor, and turn aside the way of the meek."[2] What a picture do these few words suggest to us of society in the Northern Kingdom, 750 years before Christ, and of the faculty for keen and comprehensive criticism possessed by the herdman from Tekoa! Amos, the first of the canonical prophets, transcends the bounds of Jewish particularism : he never, it has been noticed, describes Jehovah as the God of Israel ; he describes him as the "God of Hosts," which, whatever the origin of the phrase may have been,[3] becomes practically equivalent to the Omnipotent : and here he represents Him as meting out equal justice, alike to Israel and the Gentiles, not for the neglect of religious rites, not even for their adhesion to unspiritual service,

---

[1] Amos i. 2—ii. 5.   [2] Amos ii. 6-7.
[3] Comp. E. Kautzsch, in Herzog's *Real-Encyklopädie* (ed. 2), art. *Zebaoth* (1886) : and in Stade's *Zeitschrift für die alttestamentliche Wissenschaft*, 1886, p. 17 ff.

but for their repudiation of the duties and offices imposed upon all by their common humanity. Amos' keen sense of justice appears again and again in the course of his prophecy. Thrice does Jehovah swear:[1] and each time the oath is elicited by some deed of selfishness, or indifference, or dishonesty: "Hear this, ye that would swallow up the needy, and make the poor of the land to fail; saying, When will the new moon be gone, that we may sell corn? and the Sabbath, that we may set forth wheat? making the ephah small and the shekel great, and falsifying the balances by deceit. . . . Jehovah hath sworn by the excellency of Jacob: Surely I will never forget any of their works."[2] And noting the inconsistency of elaborate religious observances conjoined with a disregard of the moral principles of which they should be the accompaniment and the expression, he exclaims, speaking still in Jehovah's name: "I hate, I reject your pilgrimages; and I will take no delight in your solemn assemblies. Take thou away from me the noise of thy songs; for I will not hear the melody of thy viols. But let judgment roll down as waters, and righteousness as an ever-flowing stream."[3]

In Isaiah, consistently with the more permanent and influential position enjoyed by the prophet in Jerusalem, the indictment is more detailed, and covers a wider area than is the case in Amos. His fifth

[1] Amos iv. 2, vi. 8, viii. 7.   [2] Amos viii. 4-7.
[3] Amos v. 21, 23, 24. Comp., on the prophetic work of Amos, the excellent account contained in W. R. Smith's *Prophets of Israel*, p. 120 ff.

chapter may be taken as a representative one. Opening with the parable of the vineyard, the prophet shows how, in spite of the advantages lavished profusely upon it, Israel has disappointed its Owner, and not repaid the care bestowed upon it:—"He hoped for justice, but behold bloodshed; for righteousness, but behold a cry." And then one by one the national sins are summed up.[1] The inordinate desire for the possession of large estates which now asserted itself, accompanied, no doubt, by the unfair or violent ejectment of less fortunate possessors[2]; the immoderate indulgence in pleasures of the table, leaving, in the minds of many, no room for more serious thought;[3] the devotion to sin for sin's sake, attended by a scoffing and defiant unbelief[4]; the confusion of moral distinctions, blinding men to the true nature and issue of the course which they were pursuing; the self-satisfied astuteness of the leading politicians, who were confident in the wisdom of their plans, and conceived that their projects for the welfare of the

[1] Is. v. 8-23.   [2] Comp. Mic. ii. 2.
[3] Is. v. 12^b: the "work of the LORD" and the "operation of his hands" (cf. Ps. xxviii. 5), *i.e.* the purpose of God, realizing itself in history, and by means of the laws which govern the welfare of nations. These laws, the leaders of the nation do not regard or understand: the consequence is, that the people suffer (*v.* 13).
[4] Is. v. 18: "Who draw iniquity with cords of vanity, and sin as it were with a cart rope," *i.e.* who are so devoted to sin that they chain themselves by cords of illusion, *i.e.* by worthless considerations to which they attach a fictitious importance, and drag it after them as though they were beasts of burden.

State were above criticism;[1] the systematized corruption of the administrators of justice—these are the sins which Isaiah denounces in his long invective, showing how in truth they were already working their normal effects in the deterioration of the national life,[2] incapacitating it for dealing effectually with the difficulties which the age brought with it. And if we read the volume of his prophecies as a whole, we see how no class in the community is exempted from his censure. The men of rank and authority, who ignored the responsibilities of office or position;[3] the leaders of opinion, who possessed weight in the Government, or gave a tone to society;[4] the advocates of a plausible but short-sighted policy, who possessed the art of securing the ear of the people;[5] a powerful minister whose influence he perceived was operating to the jeopardy of the State;[6] the masses whom he saw sunk in indifference or formalism;[7] the King himself, whether it were Ahaz in his wilfulness

[1] Is. v. 21. In illustration of the "wisdom" here alluded to, comp. xxix. 14^b; xxxi. 2^a: "He also—*i. e.* Jehovah, not less than the politicians—is wise, and doth not recall his words," &c.
[2] Is. v. 24. Notice the figures employed. The image is that of a tree, rotting where it stands: the "root," which ought to be the channel of nutriment, becomes rottenness, and the "blossom," which ought to be fresh and healthy, vanishes in the air as dust. And so the collapsing strength of the nation is compared by the prophet to a mass of hay sinking down and disappearing rapidly in the flames.
[3] i. 23; iii. 14-15; xxviii. 7 f.; xxix. 20 f.   [4] iii. 12.
[5] xxviii. 14-22; xxix. 14^b, 15 f.; xxx. 1-3, 7 ff.; xxxi. 1 f.
[6] xxii. 15 ff.
[7] i. 4, 10 ff.; ii. 6 ff.; xxix. 13 f.; xxx. 8-11; xxxii. 9 ff.

and insincerity, or Hezekiah listening incautiously to the overtures of a foreign potentate[1]—all in turn receive the prophet's bold and fearless rebuke. In Isaiah, we have an example of the prophet, upon a more conspicuous and broader platform than that on which Amos stood, engaged in a lifelong conflict with the dominant tendencies of his age.

I have sought to illustrate, under two aspects, the historical significance of the prophets. History, we see, elucidates the prophecy; prophecy interprets the history. If we would understand the prophecy rightly, we must throw ourselves back to the time at which it was uttered, and realize the social and political situation to which it was addressed. Then, in its turn, prophecy illumines, and even directs, the history. May the Spirit which quickened and exalted the genius of the prophets help us, as we read their writings, to take the lessons which they teach to ourselves! May He inspire us, if it be possible, with the same generous and disinterested impulses, the same lofty aspirations, the same admiration of nobility in thought and deed, the same honesty and love of truth!

[1] vii. 10 ff. ; xxxix. 3 ff.

SERMON VI.[1]

THE VOICE OF GOD IN THE OLD TESTAMENT.

Heb. i. 1-2 : "God, having of old time spoken unto the fathers in the prophets, by divers portions and in divers manners, hath at the end of these days spoken unto us in his Son."

THE Epistle to the Hebrews opens in the Greek with two significant adverbs, πολυμερῶς and πολυτρόπως, which the writer uses for the purpose of characterizing the revelation contained in the Old Testament. The first of these adverbs is one which it is difficult to reproduce in our language at once forcibly and idiomatically. Perhaps the sense expressed by it will be best understood if we recollect that it is opposed to ἀμερῶς, which would denote *singly, undividedly;* and that it thus conveys the idea of what, instead of being single and undivided, is broken into many parts. If we might illustrate the Apostle's meaning by a metaphor, we might say that he represents God's former revelation as not concentrated in a single volume, or mediated by a single agent, but as distributed through many channels, and mediated by a

[1] Preached at Great St. Mary's, Cambridge, before the University, on Sunday, April 27, 1890.

succession of different agents. In the use of the term it is, moreover, indirectly involved that the individual agents in whom God thus severally spake, received but a partial—we might almost say a fragmentary—revelation of His will. Πολυτρόπως, the other adverb which the writer of the Epistle uses, is explained more readily : it indicates simply diversity of manner, "in many modes." The same two adverbs are used, as it happens, in combination by Clement of Alexandria,[1] in illustration of the epithet πολυποίκιλος applied by St. Paul to the wisdom of God in Eph. iii. 10, which displays itself, this father says, "for our advantage 'in many parts and in many modes,' in art, in knowledge, in faith, in prophecy." It is the manifold and multiform manifestation of God, received of old by the fathers through the prophets, which the Apostle here describes, and with which he contrasts the single and supreme revelation made "at the end of these days," in One who was no prophet, or other subordinate minister, but "a son."

I propose to offer for your consideration to-day some reflections, suggested by these words of the Apostle, on the variety of form and circumstance and occasion, with which, as recorded in the Old Testament, God revealed Himself to the fathers. And first and foremost He revealed Himself to them in the prophets properly so called. With but few exceptions, it is only the prophets who make the claim to announce God's "word," to enunciate a

[1] Quoted by Dr. Westcott, in his note *ad. loc.*

THE VOICE OF GOD IN THE OLD TESTAMENT. 121

message which they have received from Him. The prophet is in a peculiar sense the organ of Jehovah's will. He has listened in the council of the Almighty;[1] he has stood, in vision, in the presence-chamber of the Most High, and heard there words which thrilled through his inmost being;[2] he has felt within him the impulse, before which he quailed as at the lion's roar, or which consumed his bones as a hidden fire;[3] he knows that Jehovah "doeth nothing but he revealeth his secret to his servants the prophets;"[4] ever and anon, as he speaks, it is "Thus saith Jehovah," "Hear ye the word of Jehovah," "'Tis the oracle of Jehovah." If there are degrees of inspiration, the highest degree must surely be sought in those who thus constantly and unwaveringly declare the plenitude of their inspiration, and claim to bring directly to men the message of the Most High. But the prophets did not always receive this message through the same activity of their mental organism. Sometimes they became conscious of it in a vision;[5] more frequently, as it would seem, by an impulse or direction given to their waking thoughts, or by a quickening of their natural faculties of intuition or reflection. And their message, when received, was communicated to men in many different forms. Sometimes it was expressed in plain, direct language;

---

[1] Jer. xxiii. 18, 22. [2] Is. vi. 1-13.
[3] Amos iii. 8, Jer. xx. 9. [4] Amos iii. 7.
[5] 1 Kings xxii. 19-22, Amos vii. 1-9, viii. 1-3, ix. 1-4, Hos. xii. 12, Is. vi., Jer. i., xxiv. 1-3, Ezek. i., &c.

sometimes it was made palpable in a significant act;[1] more often it was clothed by the prophet's imagination in the gorgeous dress of poetic symbolism. In genius and character the individual prophets differ widely: but they all possess, in a rare degree, the power of presenting their thought in an attractive literary garb. The flowing periods of Amos, the condensed vehemence of Hosea, the majestic oratory of Isaiah, the artless pathos of Jeremiah, the studied pictures of Ezekiel, the warm and impassioned eloquence of the great prophet of the exile—all, in different ways, while they reflect the diversified individuality of their authors, at the same time excite profoundly the reader's interest and attention.

Nor are the topics with which the prophets deal less varied than their styles. The prophets come to the forefront in many capacities. They move with the times, and are the representatives of the best thought and of the best culture which the Israelitish nation could produce. Politically, they are their nation's truest counsellors at the critical moments of its history. In earlier times they are influential in setting up or dethroning dynasties: at a later time they stand beside the king to admonish or advise. They saw more clearly than their contemporaries, as the result repeatedly showed, the bearing upon Israel of the movements and tendencies operative about them: they interpreted beforehand the signs of the

---

[1] *E. g.* Is. xx., Jer. xiii. 1-11, xix. 10 f., xxvii. 2, xxviii. 10, li. 59-64, Ezek. xii. 1 ff., xxxvii. 15-20.

THE VOICE OF GOD IN THE OLD TESTAMENT. 123

times, and warned their countrymen how to face the future. With what clear insight do Amos and Hosea detect the germs of dissolution in the fabric of the Northern Kingdom! How confidently and how unerringly does Isaiah declare, first the failure of Syria and Ephraim, then the failure of those more formidable aggressors, the Assyrians, in their projects for the ruin of Judah! With what a just instinct does he plant his finger upon the hollowness of Egyptian promises![1] And how truly a century afterwards does Jeremiah, apparently in direct antagonism to the line pursued by his great predecessor, foresee the success of the Chaldæans, and divine the purpose of Providence to crown Nebuchadnezzar as the monarch of Western Asia![2] And yet another prophet, still in advance of his contemporaries, when the appointed term of the Babylonian empire was approaching, heralded the advent of the conqueror who was to overthrow it,[3] sustained with glowing promises the failing spirits of his countrymen, and sketched in grand, imposing outline his nation's future destiny. From the time of Moses onwards, at every important epoch in the history of Israel, it was a prophet who assumed the place of authority, and taught his people the duty which the age required of it.

But the prophets were more than political counsellors: they were the chief upholders of morality

[1] Is. xx. 5, 6, xxx. 5, 7, xxxi. 3.
[2] Jer. xxv. 8-11, 15-29, xxvii. 6, 8-11 : comp. above, p. 104 f.
[3] Is. xli. 2, 25, xliv. 28, xlv. 1-4, 13, &c.

SERMON VI.

and religion. Not only did they uphold generally, in accents of solemn earnestness which can never lose their spell, the claims of righteousness, philanthropy, equity, and other social virtues—so apt in all countries, but especially in Eastern countries, to be disregarded—and the claims of Jehovah as against other gods whose worship possessed often such a strange attractiveness for the less spiritually minded Israelites; but they taught also many special lessons. Amos, for instance, teaches the impartiality with which God views all nations, and shows that he demands of Israel precisely the same standard of equity and right which he exacts of other nations.[1] Hosea, the prophet of religious emotion, teaches the love with which Jehovah regards Israel, and while reproaching Israel for the imperfect manner in which His love was requited by it, deduces the lesson that the individual Israelite who seeks to participate in God's love, must show love, on his own part, to his brother man.[2] Isaiah, in imagery of which he alone is master, sets forth the majesty of Jehovah's Godhead, declares the triumph of righteousness and true religion in the overthrow of the Assyrian, and holds up before his nation the inspiring ideals of a renovated human nature, a purified and transformed society.[3] Ezekiel, while watching from his distant

---

[1] Amos ii. 6-8 (cf. i. 3—ii. 5), ix. 7-10. Comp. pp. 114-116.
[2] Hos. xi. 1-4; ii. 2-5, 8, iii. 1, iv. 1, 2, vi. 4-7, xii. 6.
[3] Is. x. 5-23; i. 26, ii. 2-4, iv. 3-4, xxix. 17-24, xxx. 20-22, xxxii. 1-8, 15-18, xxxiii. 5-6, 24.

THE VOICE OF GOD IN THE OLD TESTAMENT. 125

exile's home the toils closing around Jerusalem,[1] asserts, in uncompromising stringency, the doctrine of individual responsibility,[2] and vindicates—though in a very different manner from Isaiah—the majesty of Jehovah, which might seem to have been disparaged by the disastrous ruin of the city of His choice.[3] And the prophet to whom I have already alluded as heralding the advent of Cyrus, preaches, in language more exalted and impressive than is to be found in any other part of the Bible, the transcendence, the omnipotence, the infinitude of Israel's God, His incomparable and incommunicable Being, and withal His purposes of salvation, which, though they are directed with special affection towards Israel, comprehend within their ultimate scope all the kindreds of the earth.[4] In the approaching restoration of the exiled nation, he sees, what Ezekiel did not see, an event of crucial significance in the history of the world, and one adapted in the end to create a revolution in the religious feelings of mankind.[5] In the case of every prophet, the message, which it is distinctively his to bring, is correlated partly with his individual character and genius, partly with the circumstances and history of his age. And thus in

[1] Ezek. i.-xxiv.
[2] Ezek. xviii.
[3] Ezek. xxxvi. 20-24, 36, xxxviii. 23, xxxix. 7, 21-24. Comp. Prof. A. B. Davidson's *Ezekiel*, in the *Cambridge Bible for Schools*, pp. xxxix-xlii.
[4] Is. xliv. 5, xlv. 14, 23, lii. 10.
[5] Is. xl. 5, xlii. 1^b ("judgment" = religion), 3^b, 4^b, xlv. 6, xlix. 6, li. 4, lvi. 7, 8, lxvi. 23 (comp. the writer's *Isaiah*, p. 168 ff.).

many parts and in many modes did God speak to the fathers in the prophets.

The historical books describe another aspect of God's dealings with His people; they narrate from different points of view, and with different degrees of historical precision, Israel's chequered history,—the story how from small beginnings and through many vicissitudes it rose to be an organized nation, able to hold its own among its neighbours, shorn of part of its glory by the Assyrians, but succumbing finally only to the Chaldæans, and then wonderfully restored to its ancient home in order to complete its destined course of history. Providence watched over Israel's path, and guided the hands of its leading men. And the history, as it is told, is penetrated from the beginning with religious ideas. The narrative of the Creation sets forth, in a series of dignified and impressive pictures, the sovereignty of God; His priority to, and separation from, all finite, material nature; His purpose to constitute an ordered cosmos; His endowment of man with the peculiar, unique possession of self-conscious reason, in virtue of which he becomes capable of intellectual and moral life, and is even able to hold communion with his Maker. The story of the Fall shows how human wilfulness thwarted God's purpose in regard to the future of man, and introduced into the world moral disorder. The account of the Flood becomes a typical illustration of God's anger against sin, as the covenant formed by him with Noah evinces the gracious regard with

THE VOICE OF GOD IN THE OLD TESTAMENT. 127

which, if they would but respond, He views the whole race of mankind. In the narratives which follow, although it is probable that we have mostly traditions rather than the testimony of eye-witnesses, both the contents and the animating spirit are not less remarkable. In the history of the patriarchs we have the picture of men, who, in that distant age, are witnesses and examples of a lively faith to those of other nations with whom they come in contact, and who, while moving about with their flocks and their herds, and though drawn by their wives and children and family connexions into various entanglements, are still the founders of a religious community: "For I have known him, to the end that he may command his children and his household after him, that they may keep the way of the LORD, to do justice and judgment."[1] The patriarchs are engaged in founding not one of the empires of the world, but a kingdom of which righteousness is to be the rule. The ideal character and aims of the people of God are prefigured in their history. It is the religious colouring of the narrative which impresses us, the didactic aim which, apparently unsought for, nevertheless attaches to it. The story of Israel's ancestors might have been told very differently. The religious spirit might have been absent from it altogether. As it is, the patriarchs are types of religious characters; and their lives abound with lessons for ourselves.

Nor is the case different afterwards. In the Mosaic

[1] Gen. xviii. 19.

age the conspicuous figure is the character of Moses himself. The character of Moses is sketched with peculiar vividness and force: he is represented as endowed, in a pre-eminent degree, with singleness of aim, with nobility of mind, with unwearied and self-sacrificing devotion for the welfare of his people, and with that modesty both of word and demeanour which is observable in all the best characters of Old Testament history. Hosea styles him a prophet[1]: prophetic insight and foresight are ascribed to him in the Pentateuch: Jehovah is represented as holding converse with him not by a vision or a dream, but with some special and distinctive clearness, "as a man speaketh unto his friend."[2] To the period while Israel was at Sinai, there is referred the re-affirmation of the aim of Israel's national existence, which was foreshadowed in the history of Abraham: "Now, therefore, if ye will obey my voice indeed, and keep my covenant, then ye shall be a peculiar treasure to me above all peoples: for all the earth is mine: and ye shall be unto me a kingdom of priests and an holy nation."[3] To Moses, in a supreme moment of his life, is vouchsafed the manifestation of Jehovah's gracious character, which dominates Israel's history, and which prophets and psalmists, one after another, re-echo: "And the LORD passed by before him, and proclaimed, Jehovah, Jehovah, a God merciful and

---

[1] Hos. xii. 13.
[2] Ex. xxxiii. 11; cf. Num. xii. 8, Deut. xxxiv. 10.
[3] Ex. xix. 5-6.

gracious, long-suffering and abundant in goodness and faithfulness; keeping mercy for thousands, forgiving iniquity and transgression and sin: and that will by no means clear the guilty; visiting the iniquity of the fathers upon the children, and upon the children's children, upon the third and upon the fourth generation. And Moses made haste, and bowed his head toward the earth and worshipped."[1] To Moses are attributed the words which with a burst of grateful enthusiasm celebrate the theocratic privileges of the Chosen People: "There is none like unto God, O Jeshurun, who rideth upon the heaven as thy help and in his majesty on the skies . . . Happy art thou, O Israel: who is like unto thee, a people saved by the LORD, the shield of thy help, and that is the sword of thy majesty! and thine enemies shall submit themselves unto thee; and thou shall tread upon their high places."[2] Upon all the pictures which we possess of the Mosaic age, there is impressed a profound consciousness of Israel's vocation, of the duties imposed upon it, and of the privileges which it enjoys.

In the Law of Moses, God speaks in different ways; and we hear His voice accommodating itself to the needs of different ages, and of different classes of men. In one group of laws[3] the needs of a simple, comparatively immature, agricultural society appear to be held in view. While the Decalogue[4] embodies

[1] Ex. xxxiv. 6-8. [2] Deut. xxxiii. 26-29.
[3] Ex. xx. 23—xxiii. 33. [4] Ex. xx. 1-17.

the fundamental maxims of man's duty towards God and his neighbour, such as are valid while human nature remains the same, the group of laws following it regulates such subjects as slavery, the rights of neighbours possessing contiguous fields and pastures, compensation for injury to life or limb, cases of damage to property; and prescribe [1] rudimentary principles of sacrifice and religious worship. One or two of the provisions strike us as harsh; and certainly, when applied literally, in ages deficient in the historical instinct, to altered conditions of society, these have sometimes led to disastrous consequences; but side by side with them we are sensible of an atmosphere of true philanthropy, and in one instance, note the anticipation, in a form suited to the time, of a genuinely Christian spirit, in the injunction, viz., not to refuse help to an enemy in his need—" If thou meet thine enemy's ox or his ass going astray, thou shalt surely bring it back to him again. If thou see the ass of him that hateth thee lying under his burden thou shalt forbear to leave it to him alone; thou shalt surely loosen it with him."[2] In another group of laws, those embodied in Deuteronomy, the requirements of a more advanced society are contemplated: the provisions of the code embrace more complicated relations of life; great stress is laid upon the moral and religious motives which should prompt obedience

---

[1] Ex. xx. 23-26, xxii. 20, xxiii. 13, 14-19, 24; cf. the repetition of many of these laws in Ex xxxiv. 10-26.
[2] Ex. xxiii. 4-5.

to them; the spiritual teaching is higher and more definite. In yet another group,[1] the holiness which should determine and pervade the Israelite's life is emphasized; and the principle is made the basis of a series of important moral and social obligations. And a fourth and larger group [2] regulates with some minuteness the ceremonial institutions, which as time advanced became more and more distinctly the formal expression of Israel's faith. The ceremonial system of ancient Israel has played an important function in the religious education of mankind. It enforced and deepened the sense of sin. It declared the need of restoration and forgiveness. It developed—perhaps gradually—in the form of institutions the great principles which regulate man's converse with God. It emphasized the significance of sacrifice under its different aspects, as eucharistic, dedicatory, propitiatory. It taught more and more distinctly that an atoning rite must precede the acceptance of the worshipper by God. It thus established the principles which in the fulness of time were to receive their supreme and final application in the sacrifice of Christ. In all its stages, the Mosaic law held before the eyes of Israel an ideal of duty to be observed, of

[1] Lev. xvii.-xxvi.,—called often, by modern critics, on account of the motive which principally dominates it, the "Law of Holiness." See the writer's *Introduction*, pp. 43, 44, 47.
[2] The laws forming the main stock of the "Priests' Code," and contained chiefly in Ex. xii. 1-20, 40-51, xiii. 1-2, xxv.-xxxi., Lev. i.-xvi., xxvii., Numb. v., vi., xv., xviii., xix., xxvii., xxviii.-xxix., xxx., xxxv., xxxvi.

laws to be obeyed, of principles to be maintained; it taught them that human nature needed to be restrained; it impressed upon them the necessity of discipline. And in an age when disintegrating influences might have operated disastrously upon the nation, the institutions of the law bound together the majority of its members in a religious society, strong enough to resist the forces which threatened to dissolve it. In many parts and in many modes did God, through the ordinances of the law, speak to His people, training it till it should be able to dispense with their aid, and be ready to assimilate the higher teaching of Christ. But the imperfect and provisional character of the law is, in principle, expressly recognized by our Lord, who says of one enactment that it was written "for the hardness of your hearts," and who even propounds a higher standard of action than is presented in the Decalogue itself. It thus affords a conspicuous example of God speaking to His people in language that had only a relative value, and was suited only to the needs of a particular people, and of particular times.

God spake again to the fathers through poetry, the language of the emotions, the language in which every nation has uttered some of the deepest thoughts of its heart. The poetry of the Old Testament is surpassed in its kind by none: who is insensible to the charm of its light and graceful movement, its balanced, responsive rhythm, so grateful to the ear even in a translation, the truth and force with which the scenery

THE VOICE OF GOD IN THE OLD TESTAMENT. 133

of nature or human life and character are delineated in it? It is moreover singularly varied in its themes; the Hebrew poets speak in many strains and in many moods. We hear fragments of the martial lyrics in which national victories or the deeds of national heroes were celebrated by the nation's poets;[1] and more than one triumphal ode in which the nation or an individual renders thanks for the deliverance vouchsafed by Jehovah has been preserved complete.[2] We have the dramatic poem, in which by the interchange of argument a great problem of human life is illustrated on its different sides, and the reader is thus gradually led up to the truth which the poet desires finally to unfold. We have, at least in a rudimentary form, the drama itself, in the Song of Songs, where with rare delicacy of language, and beauty of figure and of thought, there is represented the triumph of faithful love over the blandishments of a monarch and the attractions of a gilded court. We have the elegy, in which the poet in accents of tenderness bewails his lost friend,[3] or speaking on behalf of his nation dwells pathetically upon its sufferings, appeals beseechingly to the Divine compassion, and ends with the assurance of restoration to come.[4] We have gnomic poetry, founded, as it seems, by the wise king Solomon, cultivated after

---

[1] Numb. xxi. 14 f., 27-30, Josh. x. 12^b-13^a; cf. Ps. lxviii. 11-14; also 1 Sam. xviii. 7 (cf. xxi. 11).
[2] Ex. xv. 1-18, Judg. v.
[3] 2 Sam. i. 19-27; iii. 33-34.
[4] Lam. i.-v.

him by others of those shrewd observers of life and character whom Israel produced, in which the wisdom of many generations is stored up for the instruction of future ages. In the Psalter all voices of the human soul are heard. There is despondency unrelieved by any gleam of light; there is grief ending in hope, or even in a strain of thanksgiving, in confident anticipation of coming deliverance; there is distress and anguish, sometimes caused by persecuting foes, sometimes by a faithless friend, sometimes resulting from sickness, sometimes produced by the consciousness of sin; there are psalms of faith and resignation, of rejoicing and jubilation, of yearning for God's presence, and the spiritual privilege of communion with Him; there are didactic psalms, psalms deducing lessons from the past, or meditating on the problems and contradictions of the present; there are psalms echoing national calamities or successes; there is the cry of penitence wrung from the nation's heart by the bitter experiences of exile; there is its new-born consciousness of a wider and more glorious future in store for it, in the psalms which declare that "Jehovah reigneth";[1] there are prophetic outlooks into the future;[2] there are medi-

---

[1] Ps. xciii., xcvi., xcvii., xcix.; cf. Ps. xlvii., xcviii. All these Psalms breathe the same spirit, and may be regarded as the lyric echo of Is. xl.-lxvi. With "Jehovah reigneth" comp. Is. lii. 7b. Comp. further Ps. xciii. 1 with Is. li. 9; xcvi. 1, 11 with Is. xlii. 10, xlix. 13; xcviii. 1-4 with Is. xlii. 10, lii. 10, lxiii 5, 7, xliv. 23; xcviii. 7, 8 with Is. xlii. 10, lv. 12, &c.

[2] Cf. Ps. xxii. 22-31, xlvii. 9, lxv. 2, lxviii. 28-35, lxxxvi. 9, cii. 21-22.

tations on the power and goodness of God as shown in creation, in history, in His dealings with the human race and with Israel. In the Psalms the devotional element of the religious character finds its completest expression; and the soul is displayed in converse with God, disclosing to Him its manifold emotions, desires, aspirations. It is the surprising variety of mood, and subject, and occasion in the Psalms, which gives them their catholicity, and fits them to be the hymn-book not of the second Temple only, but of the Christian Church. In the Psalms we hear the voices of many different men, possessed of different temperaments, moving in the midst of different circumstances, and living at very different periods of the nation's life. But national history was the instrument which in God's hand struck the keynote of the deepest utterances of the psalmist, not less than of the prophet, in ancient Israel.

And thus in many parts and many modes did the voice of God speak unto the fathers in the prophets. Yet we must not suppose that it spoke in them mechanically: the prophet was not, what the Greek μάντις was imagined to be, the unintelligent medium through which truth from another world was communicated to man. The psychical conditions under which God spoke in them, the nature and operation of the initial impulse which brought them to the consciousness of Divine truth, may belong to those secrets of man's inner life which God has reserved to Himself: but by whatever means this consciousness was aroused, the Divine element which it contained was assimilated by the prophet, and thus appears blended with the elements that were the expression of his own character and genius. The Divine thought takes shape in the soul of the prophet, and is presented to us, so to speak, in the garb and imagery with which he has invested it; it is expressed in terms which bear the external marks of his own individuality, and reflect the circumstances of time and place and other similar conditions, under which it was first propounded. Divine truth is always presented through the human organ; it is always though doubtless not always to the same degree, coloured by the medium through which it has been transmitted. The Divine and the human elements are inseparably blended, and not, as it would seem, in every part of the Old Testament in precisely the same proportions. The material data contained in the historical books lay no claim to be derived from other than human sources; and there are at least portions of the same books, the spiritual value of which is not as great as that of the Prophets or the Psalms. Nor can it be denied that there are parts of the Old Testament in which a personal, or national, temper asserts itself in a spirit which is not that of Christ. And if, moreover, it be true that in the religion of Israel that which is perfect is not yet attained, but is only in process of being reached, then, as the venerable Delitzsch has remarked in his last work,[1]

[1] *Messianische Weissagungen* (1890), p. 20.

it ought not to offend us even should the Old Testament Scriptures prove to contain more elements that are relatively imperfect than has hitherto been supposed to be the case.

But viewed generally the human element, whether it be present in a larger or smaller proportion, is interpenetrated and suffused by an element higher than itself; it is illumined, elevated, and refined by a peculiar and unique operation of the Spirit of God. True and noble thoughts gleam like flashes of light from the pages of the great thinkers of ancient Greece; the labours of modern scholars have disclosed to us the forms of those searchers after truth, who in a remote past, and in distant climes, felt after God, and in part also found Him (for " he left not himself without witness " among men): but the voices of these men are dim and faltering, as compared with the clear and vivid consciousness of truth which is reflected in every part of the Old Testament; and the truths which they reached contrast strongly, in respect of fulness, warmth, and richness, with those which are enunciated by the prophets and poets of ancient Israel. These writers speak from a soul that has been touched, and a heart that has been warmed, by the Spirit of the living God. And that the religion of Israel, though subject in its growth to historical conditions, is not to be explained as arising solely out of them, is not, in other words, to be treated as a natural product of the genius of the people, appears besides from the fact that it stands from the beginning above the ordinary level that was reached by the nation generally: throughout its history the people are represented as needing to be taught by others, as declining from truth by which they ought to have been guided, as falling short of the ideal propounded to them. The natural tendencies of the nation did not move in the direction of spiritual religion. There is no ground to suppose that, apart from the special illumination vouchsafed to the great teachers who originated, or sustained, the principles of its faith, the religious history of Israel would have differed materially from that of the kindred nations by which it was surrounded.

I close with some thoughts, suggested by what has been said, on the permanent importance of the Old Testament. It is important in the first place, on account of the revelation which it contains of the character of God, Who is represented in it as a personal Being, Who, though depicted under the most vivid anthropomorphic imagery, is nevertheless conceived always as purely spiritual, is never confused either with the world or with material emblems of His presence; Who possesses a definite moral character, all-holy, all-just, all-wise; Who condescends to enter into relations of grace with His intelligent creatures; Who loves man and will in turn be loved by him; Whose anger is aroused by sin, but Who is gracious to the repentant sinner; Who manifests Himself in His redemptive purpose to Israel, and designs in the future to manifest Himself to other nations as well; Who leads His nation step by step, as with a father's hand, through joy and sorrow, through success and disappointment, through victory and defeat, to know Him better, and to learn His character more clearly.

Secondly, the Old Testament sets before us an ideal of human character; it stimulates us by many a noble example of faith and action. Of course the characters which it brings before us are not faultless; some are held up as warnings; in the case of others, it is evident, their faults are fewer and less grave than they would have been, had they lived where the purifying and mellowing influence of the religion of Israel could not have reached them. Even in the prehistoric and patriarchal ages the principal characters are so delineated as to be typically significant; they constitute examples to be either imitated or shunned. In a later age we see a man like David, endowed with high personal qualities, amiable, generous, disinterested, loyal, "a born ruler of men," in spite of the occasion of his great fall, and in spite also of some other occasions on which he was not superior to the spirit of his age—manifesting in his demeanour and actions generally the softening influence of his religion.[1] We see in a book like Ruth religion operative in a lowlier sphere, sanctifying and elevating the

---

[1] On the character of David, comp. the just and appreciative remarks of Prof. W. R. Smith in the *Encyclopædia Britannica*, art. "David" (1877), p. 841; and Prof. T. K. Cheyne, *Aids to the Devout Study of Criticism* (1892), pp. 16-73 (esp. pp. 67-70).

ordinary duties of life. We see exemplified in the prophets sincerity of purpose, uncompromising opposition to vice and sin, constant devotion to principle, firm faith in a higher power. We see, as I have already said, the devotional temper, under many different aspects, exemplified in the Book of Psalms. The religion of the Old Testament produced a type of character which, though it may have lacked the finer graces which the teaching and example of Christ produced, is one which we may all strive to imitate. Naturally our judgment upon individuals must be controlled by the absolute principles of conduct recognized by the Old Testament itself; nor must we forget that in some respects the circumstances of ancient Israel were different from ours, so that maxims of action beyond the pale of what is moral and spiritual, cannot be transferred immediately to ourselves: but in its predominant features human nature is the same in all ages; so that the lesson as a rule can be applied directly.

Thirdly, the Old Testament has an intimate and important bearing upon the Christian faith. As a matter of history, Judaism was the cradle of Christianity. Viewed humanly, Christianity in its origin took the form of a reaction against the paralyzing influences of Rabbinism, a reaction resting primarily upon a return to the more spiritual religion of the prophets—a call of which the first note was struck by John the Baptist, the "heir of the prophets." I am speaking of it in its initial stage: of course many fresh elements were added afterwards. But although Christianity was thus a reaction against the unspiritual developments of the later legalism, it does not need to be pointed out how deeply its roots were laid in the ancient faith of Israel, what vital doctrines it appropriated from Israel's teaching, and took for granted ; or how the long and gradual preparation of history fitted the soil for its growth. Of the elements forming the preparation in history for Christ, while some, it is true, were contributed from other quarters, those of central and material importance were supplied by the religion of the Old Testament.

The Old Testament is also of importance, for us, evidentially. When all deductions which exegetical and critical honesty demands have been made, it is impossible to overlook or deny the correspondence subsisting between the anticipations and ideals of Israel and their fulfilment in Christ. It is remarkable how, while most nations placed their visions of perfection in the past and looked back sorrowfully to a golden age which had passed for ever away, the Jews uniformly looked forward : how their most representative men expressed expectations which nothing in their own age satisfied; how they held out, and adhered to, ideals which remained unrealized ; how, heedless of the irony of history, they still projected the image of a changed social state; how they proclaimed the advent of a Prophet and of a King, who by the supreme graces of his person, and the superhuman qualities of his rule, should transform and regenerate human nature; how they announced confidently the future abolition of restrictions which the principles of their own religion appeared to treat as permanently valid. The prophets shadow forth a *summum bonum*, transcending experience, in which the Gentiles are to participate equally with the Chosen People, and which they believe is destined assuredly to be realized. And when we look more closely we perceive that distinct lines of prophecy and type converge upon Christ, and He fulfils them. In Him the ideals, flung forth with magnificent profusion upon the pages of the Old Testament, are gathered up and realized. Special predictions are indeed sometimes doubtful exegetically, sometimes capable of being otherwise explained; but there is one truth writ too large in the Bible to be obliterated or debated, that the Old Testament exhibits the development, by successive stages, of a grand redemptive purpose, and that the New Testament records its completion. In the Gospel the principles inchoate in the Old Testament are matured; in the kingdom which Christ has founded the aims and aspirations of the great teachers of Israel are satisfied and fulfilled.

SERMON VII.[1]

INSPIRATION.

Tim. iii. 16-17 : " Every scripture inspired of God is also profitable for teaching, for reproof, for correction, for instruction which is in righteousness : that the man of God may be complete, furnished completely unto every good work."

THESE words apply primarily to the Old Testament. This appears not only from the fact that at the time when they were written the New Testament was still incomplete, and the writings which existed could hardly have acquired the recognized authority implied in this connection by the Greek term γραφή, but also from considerations arising out of the context. In the preceding verses the Apostle urges Timothy to abide in the things which he has learned, and been assured of, knowing of whom he has learned them, that "from a babe thou hast known the sacred writings which are able to make thee wise unto salvation through faith which is in Christ Jesus." The Scriptures which Timothy, "the son of a Jewess which believed," whom Paul "took and circumcised" at

[1] Preached at St. Mary's, before the University, on Sunday, Nov. 1, 1891.

Lystra,[1] had known from a babe, could only have been those of the Old Covenant; and it is for the purpose of enforcing or illustrating the statement that these Scriptures are able to make wise unto salvation, that the Apostle proceeds with the words that I have taken as my text: "Every scripture inspired of God is also profitable for teaching, for reproof, for correction, for instruction which is in righteousness; that the man of God may be complete, furnished completely unto every good work."

The subject suggested by my text is one on which it is difficult to say anything which has not been said before. I can only invite your attention this morning to some aspects of it which, though they have been often pointed to, are still sometimes overlooked, and which it seems important to bear in mind at the present day.

"Every Scripture inspired of God." What does this expression signify? We inquire in vain for any authoritative answer. The use of the word will not guide us, for no other Biblical writer employs it. Scripture itself supplies no material assistance; for though the Biblical writers often assert the Divine origin of particular declarations made by them, there is no parallel statement, speaking with greater distinctness, respecting the origin of the Bible as a whole. Our Church in its formularies treats the Scriptures as the authoritative rule of faith, and is careful to emphasize their sufficiency unto salvation: but it has

---

[1] Acts xvi. 1, 3.

INSPIRATION.

given no definition of inspiration; and the books constituting Holy Scripture are described solely by the external mark of being canonical, not by any internal character or quality affirmed to inhere in them. Nevertheless men have assumed that they knew, as it were, intuitively what inspiration meant, and what it involved: they have framed theories of its nature accordingly, and have demanded that the Bible should conform to them. Some, for instance, have imagined inspiration to imply the complete suspension of the human personality, so that the inspired agent resembled a flute in the hands of a player. Others, not going quite so far as this, have still not been able to conceive of inspiration, except as determining the very words and letters of the Bible. Everything, these divines have said, written under inspiration is in every particular and in every relation infallible. "The affirmations of Scripture of all kinds, whether of spiritual doctrine or duty, or of physical or historical fact, or of psychological or philosophical principle, are without any error when the *ipsissima verba* of the original autographs are ascertained and interpreted in their natural and intended sense." "A proved error in Scripture contradicts not only our doctrine but the Scripture claims, and therefore its inspiration in making these claims."[1] The sentences which I have quoted are

[1] Drs. Hodge and Warfield, in a joint article in the *Presbyterian Review*, 1881, pp. 238, 245. Quoted by Ll. J. Evans and H. P. Smith, *Biblical Scholarship and Inspiration* (Cincinnati, 1891), pp. 10, 12, 92 f.

not indeed from the pen of an Anglican Divine ; but they hardly do more than give pointed expression to a feeling which probably has often been shared by members of our own communion. It is important to observe that for the statements contained in them there is no warrant either in the Bible itself, or in the formularies of our Church. They are the speculations of individual theologians, framed upon the basis of *à priori* conceptions respecting what an inspired book must be, the more serious consideration, what its claims and characteristics actually are, being left out of sight altogether. It cannot be too often repeated that the only legitimate method of determining what is involved in the idea of inspiration, or under what conditions it manifests itself, is by an examination of the books that are described as inspired, and an impartial study of the facts presented by them. The Scriptures nowhere make the claim of absolute and universal inerrancy. And the characteristics of the books comprising them are in many cases very different from those which would naturally be inferred from the first of the statements which I have just read.

Without pretending to define inspiration, or to determine the mystery of its operation, we may, I suppose, say that what we mean by it is an influence which gave to those who received it a unique and extraordinary *spiritual insight*, enabling them thereby, without superseding or suppressing the human faculties, but rather using them as its instruments, to declare in different degrees, and in accordance with the needs or circumstances of particular ages or particular occasions, the mind and purpose of God. Every true and noble thought of man is indeed, in a sense, inspired of God; but with the Biblical writers the purifying and illumining Spirit must have been present in some special and exceptional measure. Nevertheless, in the words of the prophet, or other inspired writer, there is a human element, not less than a Divine element, and neither of these must be ignored. I need not pause in this place for the purpose of emphasizing the Divine element in Scripture: it is manifest to all. The "heavenliness of the matter"—to use the expressive phrase of the Westminster Confession—speaks in it with a clearness which none can mistake, and strikes a responsive chord in every heart that is open to receive a message from above. In the Old Testament we read how God awakened in His ancient people of Israel the consciousness of Himself: and we hear one writer after another unfolding different aspects of His nature, and disclosing with increasing distinctness His gracious purposes towards man. In the pages of the prophets there shine forth, with ineffaceable lustre, those sublime declarations of truth and righteousness and judgment which have impressed all readers, to whatever age or clime or creed they have belonged. In the Psalms we hear the meditations of the believing soul, contemplating with adoring wonder the manifold operations of Providence, or pouring forth its emotions in converse with God. The historians set before us, from different points of view, the successive stages in the Divine education of the race. They show us how its natural tendencies to polytheism were gradually overcome. They show us how Israel was more and more separated from its neighbours, in order to be the effectual witness and keeper of Divine truth. Sin is indeed so deeply rooted in human nature that its extirpation upon this earth is not to be expected; but the writers of the Old Testament explain to us how the ordinances of Israel were adapted to counteract its influence, and to maintain a right attitude of the heart towards God. And they interpret further their nation's history: they show us how a providential purpose dominates it; how it is subservient to God's aims; how the past leads on to better possibilities in the present; how the present points to still better possibilities in the future. And the crown and consummation of Israel's long and chequered past is set before us in the pages of the New Testament. In order to realize what the Bible is, we have but to imagine what the literature of Israel would have been, had not those to whom we owe it been illumined in some special measure by the light from heaven: even though its external history had been approximately the same, its historians, its statesmen, its essayists, its poets, would assuredly have written in a very different strain.

But though the greatness and the spiritual importance of the Divine element in Scripture has often and rightly engrossed men's attention, still, in order properly to estimate the character of the book which is termed inspired, or the revelation as we actually possess it, the human element must not be overlooked. Not only is Divine truth always presented through the human organ, and is thus, so to say, coloured by the individuality of the inspired agent by whom it is enunciated, but it is impossible to close our eyes to the fact that its enunciations are sometimes relative rather than absolute ; they are adapted to the circumstances of particular ages, they may even be limited by the spiritual capacity of the particular writer, or, in the case of his being a historian, by the materials or sources of information which he had at his disposal. The revelation of the Old Testament is avowedly progressive : the teaching in its earlier parts may naturally therefore be expected to be imperfect as compared with that which is given in its later parts, or which is to be found in the New Testament. We cannot take at random a passage from the inspired volume and say, without qualification or comparison with other passages, that it is absolute truth, or the pure word of God, or an infallible guide to conduct or character.

One or two illustrations will explain what I have in view. In the Book of Job we have a picture of the trial of the pious sufferer. Job, the patriarch of integrity and piety, is subjected to an unexampled succession of calamities. Under the weight of them he bursts forth into passionate imprecations, complaining bitterly of the misery of his lot. His friends, whose theory of life can only account for suffering as caused by some antecedent sin, accuse him wrongfully of grave offences against God and man. The patriarch, goaded to desperation by the combined severity of his sufferings and the cruel taunts of his friends, loses control of himself: he charges the Almighty with persecuting him maliciously, with treating him wilfully as guilty while He knows him to be innocent,[1] with even governing the world at large as an arbitrary and unjust despot.[2] Clearly we cannot here treat the misapplied truths placed in the mouths of the friends, or the impious sentences hurled by Job against the Almighty, as the absolute word or teaching of God. The parts of the Book of Job must be read in the light supplied by the whole: the inspiration of the poem is to be found in the manner in which the theme chosen by the poet is developed, and in the lessons which are deducible from the work as a whole. The Book of Job, treated as a whole, declares more than one great truth of God's government of the world, but it contains many particular statements, of which inerrancy cannot, in any reasonable sense of the term, be predicated.

The relativity of inspiration is observable again very noticeably in the Book of Ecclesiastes. The melancholy conclusion to which the author's moralizings lead him is, that life under all its aspects is dissatisfying and disappointing; the best that can be

---

[1] Job x. 6, 7.   [2] Job ix. 22-24; ch. xxi.

done with it is to enjoy, while it lasts, such pleasures as it brings with it. " There is nothing better for a man than that he should eat and drink, and make his soul enjoy good in his labour." [1] How strangely these words fall upon our ears! How unlike the soaring aspirations of the Psalmists, or the spirit of generous philanthropy which breathes so often in the discourses of the great prophets or the exhortations of the law! The teaching of Ecclesiastes, if followed consistently, could only result in paralyzing human effort, and stifling every impulse of an ennobling or unselfish kind. The author's theory of life is imperfect; untoward and depressing circumstances, as it seems, embittered his spirit, and concealed from him a fuller and more satisfying view of the sphere of human activity.[2] His conclusions possess only a relative value. It is upon life not absolutely, but as he witnessed and experienced it, that he passes his relentless verdict, "All is vanity." It was the particular age with which he was himself acquainted that prompted him to judge as he did of the uselessness of human endeavour; and his maxims, at least so far as they possess a negative aspect, cannot be applied to a different age without material qualification and reserve.

Even in the Psalms the same fact strikes us. Pro-

[1] Eccl. ii. 24. Comp. iii. 12, v. 18, viii. 15, where the conclusion expressed is substantially the same.
[2] Comp. Dean Bradley's helpful and suggestive *Lectures on Ecclesiastes*, 1885 (delivered originally in Westminster Abbey), p. 25 f.

found as the spirituality of the Psalms commonly is, and adequate as their language nearly at all times is to give words to the deepest religious emotions of the devout Christian, it is undeniable that passages occur in the Psalter which seem to him to strike a discordant note. It is not my intention this morning to dilate upon the so-called imprecatory Psalms, or to review the various explanations and excuses which have been offered for their presence in the Psalter: after all has been said, it must be acknowledged, in the words of the most recent commentator on the Psalms, that these utterances "belong to the spirit of the Old Testament, and not of the New Testament, and by it they must be judged."[1] Nor, though this is sometimes overlooked, do they stand alone in the Old Testament: Jeremiah more than once breaks out into invocations of vengeance against his personal enemies, which differ in no substantial respect from those which we read in the Book of Psalms.[2] And exquisite as is the pathos which breathes in the 137th Psalm, as the poet contrasts the land of his exile with his beloved ancestral home, do we not all feel the difference between his closing verse, "Happy shall he be that taketh thy little ones and dasheth them against the stones," and the words of that other Psalmist who wrote, "I will make mention of Rahab and Babylon as them that know me"?[3] It is plain

---

[1] Prof. A. F. Kirkpatrick, *The Psalms (Book I.)*, in the *Cambridge Bible for Schools and Colleges*, p. lxxv.
[2] Cf. Jer. xviii. 21-23; also xi. 20, xv. 15, xvii. 18.
[3] Ps. lxxxvii. 4.

that there exist declarations in the Bible which are not free from the tinge of human infirmity and human passage. But abundant as are the evidences of the elevating and sanctifying work of the Spirit of God upon the writers in both Testaments, we have no antecedent right to suppose that every writer is in precisely the same degree subordinated to it. Neither Scripture itself, nor the judgment of the Church, authorizes us to affirm that every statement, or even every book, stands upon the same moral or religious plane, or is in the same measure the expression of the Divine mind : the influences of time and place, of circumstances and situation, of scope and aim, of temper and opportunity, must all be taken into account, before we can rightly judge of the precise sense in which parts of Scripture are to be regarded as the word of God, and of the precise degree in which they individually claim to be authoritative.

So also there are phenomena in the historical books which are inconsistent with *à priori* theories of inspiration, as well as with hard and fast definitions of the Word of God. If there is a subject on which precision of statement might antecedently have been expected, it is surely in the record of the discourses of Christ. Yet here, while there are ample independent reasons (on which I cannot now dwell) for holding that in all essentials they have been transmitted to us faithfully, in matters of verbal exactitude no small freedom has been permitted. In the Synoptic Gospels, sayings of our Lord, in origin and occasion manifestly the same, are often presented in a more or less divergent literary form : St. Luke in particular appears to have been apt to partially recast both the narratives and the discourses which reached him, and to accommodate them to his own style. In the disposition of their materials also the Evangelists sometimes differ remarkably : matter, and to all appearance the same matter, which in one Gospel is aggregated, in another is found dispersed. The combination of resemblances and differences in the Synoptic Gospels is a most singularly literary feature ; and its explanation constitutes a problem of great perplexity, in which, though certain fixed points appear to have been gained, much still remains uncertain. But whatever solution be adopted, or even though the problem be insoluble, it is manifest that *some* editorial modification and adjustment of the material has taken place in each. And in the Fourth Gospel, a comparison with the Synoptics on the one hand, and with the Epistles of St. John on the other, makes it impossible to doubt that the actual words of Christ have often been transfused into the individuality of the Evangelist, and re-shaped in his own phraseology.[1] So far, even

[1] Comp. Archdeacon Watkins' *Bampton Lectures* (1890), p. 426 f. ; Sanday, *The Fourth Gospel*, pp. 73 f., 128-130, 222 f. ; and in *The Contemporary Review*, Oct. 1891, pp. 536, 538 f., and *The Expositor*, Nov. 1891, p. 333 ff., May 1892, p. 390 : "We are dealing [in the case of St. John] with a strong, creative personality which could not help acting upon the deposit committed to it, not a mere neutral medium through which it might pass without alteration."

in the most sacred parts of Scripture, is the truthfulness of the picture, as a whole, dissociated from the mechanical correctness of its individual parts, and made independent either of the chronological precision of the annalist, or of the verbal exactitude of the stenographist.

Nor does the Old Testament teach a different lesson. Compilation, diversity of origin, variety of motive and standpoint, are the characteristics which disclose themselves when the historical books are examined with sufficient minuteness and care. Traditions, shaped partly by oral transmission, partly by the hand of the narrator, rather than the immediate testimony of eye-witnesses, are what, it is difficult to doubt, are here sometimes presented to us. Dramatic personification, which in a more or less mature form has held such a prominent and often such an important place in the literature of the world, is seen also to be not unrepresented in the Old Testament. Why should it not be so? Why should modes and styles of composition which, except by extreme Puritans, have always been recognized as the legitimate vehicle of human thought, as well as a powerful instrument of education, be excluded from the consecrating influence of the Spirit of God? If the imagination be a faculty granted by God to man, and capable, as all must allow, of being employed in instruction and edification, why, where no fact, conditioning a theological verity, is concerned, may it not have been subordinated to the Divine plan for the spiritual advancement of the race? Where nothing is defined as to the nature or the limits of the inspiring Spirit's work, with what justice are particular spheres to be excluded, as it were upon principle, from the range of its operation? Do not the opening words of the Epistle to the Hebrews authorize us to expect variety of degree, not less than variety of form, in the manifestation of Himself which God made through the writers of the older dispensation? Through the history of Israel as a nation, through the lives of its representative men, and through the varied forms of its national literature, God has revealed Himself to the world. But this revelation was not made in its completeness at a single moment: it was subjected externally to the conditions which govern human history; it advanced progressively; and it is not more than consonant with the idea of progress that at each stage it should be regulated by the opportunities, and adapted to the capabilities, of those to whom it was primarily addressed.

Nothing is more destructive of the just claims of Christianity than a false theory of inspiration: nothing has led to more fatal shipwrecks of faith than the acceptance in youth of *à priori* views of what an inspired book must be, which the study of maturer years has demonstrated only too cogently to be untrue to fact. It needs, indeed, less than the "proved error" to confute "our doctrine": how wide an interval separates that doctrine from the "Scripture claims" with which it has been so complacently

INSPIRATION.

and yet so naïvely identified, is not, alas! always perceived. Let us, while we adhere firmly to the *fact* of inspiration, refrain from defining, and especially from limiting, the range or mode of its operation, until we have familiarized ourselves, as well as may be, with the varied contents, and with the often remarkable relations subsisting between the different parts, of the volume which we term inspired. When we have done this, it will hardly fail but that our conception of its scope will be broadened and enlarged. It seems, indeed, to be sometimes apprehended that if any modification be allowed in the popular conception of an inspired work, men's respect for the Bible will be impaired. The apprehension, though the feeling which prompts it may be sympathized with and appreciated, is surely a mistaken one. Men's respect for the Bible will be most securely won, and its authority most effectually established, by the truth about it being set before them, and by claims not being raised on its behalf *which it does not raise itself.* Men's respect for it, it is to be feared, is sometimes sadly diminished by the forced and unnatural expedients to which apologists have resorted, for the purpose of reconciling the facts which the Bible actually presents with those which, according to their own theory of its origin and contents, ought to be found in it. Shall we not do well to remember Hooker's caution: "As incredible praises given to men do often abate and impair the credit of the deserved commendation, so we must likewise take great heed lest by attributing to Scripture more than it can have, the incredibility of that do cause even those things which indeed it hath abundantly to be less reverently esteemed "?[1]

It may be doubted from this point of view whether the common use of the expression, "Word of God," as a term descriptive of the entire Bible, does not sometimes give rise to misunderstanding. To say nothing of the uncertainties of transmission, translation, and interpretation, involved in many passages, the identification of both, which it virtually implies, leaves out of sight that important aspect of the whole truth that the message from God which the Bible brings to man is always mediated through a human channel: it tends to generate a confusion between the Divine thought and the human imagery, or human form of composition, under which it is presented. The figurative language of the prophets, or the imaginative presentation of a great truth in a book like the poem of Job, will illustrate what I mean. Applied to the Bible, as a whole, the expression, "Word of God," seems to savour of the old theory of inspiration, which no one now cares to maintain, according to which the Holy Ghost dictated to the Biblical writers the very terms which they were to use: it seems to place every part of the Bible upon precisely the same spiritual level: it seems to imply an absoluteness, a finality, a perfection, which, as the instances that I have referred to sufficiently show, do

[1] *Eccl. Pol.*, II. viii. 7.

INSPIRATION.   159

not inhere in every particular statement which Scripture contains. No doubt the term could be so defined as to make it co-extensive with the whole Bible; but there would always be the danger of the technical definition being forgotten, and the popular acceptation being substituted for it. And it should be carefully remembered that this use of the term is not Biblical. In the Old Testament the term "Word of God" is applied chiefly to particular declarations of the purposes or promises of God, especially to those made by the prophets: in the New Testament it denotes commonly the gospel message, the tidings of salvation proclaimed first upon the lips of the Saviour, carried afterwards by His apostles to different quarters of the globe.[1] But it is never applied to the historical books (of either Testament), or to the Wisdom-literature, or even to the Psalms. We are thus not in a position to say whether the Biblical writers themselves would have so applied it. It is certain that no historical writer claims to draw his information from a supernatural source;[2] and it is at least worthy of consideration whether the *record* of a revelation, though legitimately termed "inspired," is itself legitimately regarded as identical with the

[1] *E. g.* Luke v. 1; Acts vi. 7, viii. 14, 25, xi. 1, xii. 24, xiii. 5, 7, 46, &c.; 1 Thess. i. 8, ii. 13; 2 Thess. iii. 1; 2 Cor. ii. 17, iv. 2.
[2] Note especially, in this connection, the preface to St. Luke's Gospel. The Evangelist, as Prof. Sanday remarks (*The Oracles of God*, p. 72), assumes no supernatural direction, he claims merely to have used the care and research that would be expected of a conscientious and painstaking historian.

"Word of God." In the official formularies of our Church there is an elasticity in the use of the expression, in strict conformity with Biblical usage—as when the priest is described not by the mechanical term of *reader*, but as the Dispenser or Preacher of God's word—which shows that it must not be treated as if it denoted solely or principally a given collection of written statements, but that it properly denotes the message sent by God to man, which may be translated into very different forms, and modified, in external representation, to suit the needs of different occasions. I venture to think that, especially in dealing with persons of limited education, it would be judicious to exercise some reserve in the use of this term, and to prefer modes of expression which, while not less just to fact, might be less open to misconstruction.[1]

But I have left unnoticed what is really the primary affirmation of my text. The context in any case,

[1] It ought perhaps to be stated distinctly, for the purpose of obviating misconception, that the remarks on the text are not intended to apply to a description of the Scriptures as "the Word of God," if accompanied by some suitable qualification such as "the Word of God, *mediated by a human agency*." Nor does the formula, which was often heard in the controversies of a past generation, "The Bible is not the Word of God, it only contains it," correspond with, or express, the writer's view. The only sense in which he regards the Scriptures as "containing" the Word of God, is that in which—if he may be allowed to adopt the simile of an old Divine, quoted by Prof. C. A. Briggs, *The Bible, the Church, and the Reason* (1892), p. 101—the lantern "contains" the light, transmitting some rays more purely and completely than others.

and, if the Revised Version be adopted, the terms of the text itself, shows that the point which the Apostle desires to emphasize is not the particular sense in which he held the Old Testament Scriptures to be inspired, but the practical teaching to be derived from them. " But abide thou in the things that thou hast learned, knowing . . . that from a babe thou hast known the sacred writings, which are able to make thee wise unto salvation through faith which is in Christ Jesus. Every Scripture inspired of God is also profitable for teaching, for reproof, for correction, for instruction which is in righteousness ; that the man of God may be complete, completely furnished unto every good work." The practical value of the Old Testament is not dependent upon a theory of the sense in which it is inspired; and those who judge the literature of Israel from what may be termed a critical as opposed to a traditional standpoint must dispute the claim, which representatives of the latter seem sometimes to make, that they alone are conscious of the worth of the Old Testament. The Old Testament Scriptures enshrine truths of permanent and universal validity. Motives, precepts, lessons, as serviceable now as they were in a distant past, start up out of its pages. In spite of the special and, it might even be said, narrowing circumstances under which they were nearly all written, in spite of the national sentiment which was a natural, and indeed a necessary, condition of the history of Israel, its great writers continually rise above all the limiting influences of time or place, and proclaim truths respecting God and man, which, as they constituted the foundation upon which the Christian faith was reared, so they have now been made the priceless and inalienable possession of humanity. We hear in the Old Testament exhortations to righteousness, and the rebuke of sin. We have set before us types for our imitation, and examples for our warning. We learn truths from it which we might in vain seek to discover for ourselves, the counsels of our Heavenly Father for the guidance of His children, the temper and frame of mind by which He would have them respond to His call. In manifold tones the Voice of God speaks to us from its pages. The Scriptures of the Old Testament are the record of a revelation, having the practical aim of raising men's thoughts towards heaven, and prompting them to righteousness and holiness of life, "that the man of God may be complete, completely furnished unto every good work." They may not exhibit the characteristics which theologians have sometimes pictured them as possessing; but if we go to them in search of the word of God, we shall infallibly find it. May we so read them that they may exert upon us the effect for which St. Paul impressed the study of them upon Timothy! May they help to furnish us completely unto every good work, and to make us wise unto salvation through faith which is in Christ Jesus!

SERMON VIII.[1]

THE FIRST CHAPTER OF GENESIS.

Job xxxviii. 4: "Where wast thou when I laid the foundations of the earth? declare, if thou hast understanding."

THE thoughts of the writers of the Old Testament turn often to the contemplation of Nature. Besides drawing from it frequent illustrations in the way of analogy or metaphor, they contemplate it more directly: they regard it sometimes in the mystery of its origin, sometimes as an ever-present declaration of the great attributes of the Creator. One writer, in the familiar chapter with which the Bible opens, prefixes to his history of the antiquities of his nation a view of the stages by which this earth was adapted to become the habitation of man. Another writer, in that unique chapter of the Book of Job from which my text is taken, meets a great moral difficulty by pointing to our imperfect acquaintance with the secrets of the physical universe, as analogous to our imperfect comprehension of the moral government of the world. The author of Psalm xix., in words

[1] Preached in the Cathedral, Christchurch, on Sunday, Nov. 29, 1885.

which the music of Haydn has made doubly familiar to us, points to the spectacle of the heavens by night as a continual witness to the work of the Divine artificer, speaking the same silent but expressive language wherever the canopy of the skies extends.[1] In Psalm civ.—that "Poem of Creation," as it has been termed—we are led to contemplate the providence by which the wants of small and great are supplied, the purposes which different objects subserve; while the countless forms of animal life are set before us as a manifestation of the Divine Spirit —"Thou hidest thy face, they are troubled; thou gatherest in their breath, they die, and return to their dust. Thou sendest forth thy spirit, they are created; and thou renewest the face of the earth."

Each of these aspects of nature would supply material for reflexion; but I propose to confine myself to-day to some thoughts suggested by the first chapter of Genesis. I need not quote its words; for in its general outline it will be familiar to all who hear me. Much has been written and said upon it— so much, indeed, that the materials for profitable consideration might well appear to be exhausted. But the subject is one of those in which every age finds a fresh interest, and by the study of which every

[1] *v.* 4: "Their line (*i.e.* the measuring-line circumscribing their domain) is gone out through all the earth, and their words unto the end of the world." The form of the comparison is as in Prov. xxv. 3, 20, 25, xxvi. 3, 14 and elsewhere (in the Hebrew, the form of all these resembles that of xxv. 3, xxvi. 3 in the English Version).

generation has something to learn. Let me therefore invite your attention to two questions connected with it. Let us inquire, firstly, Does the picture which it affords of the past history of the world agree with that which is disclosed by science? and, secondly, if it should prove that this question must be answered in the negative, What is the true value and import of the narrative? At the outset, we are met with a question of interpretation. In what sense are the six "days" spoken of in the narrative to be understood? Formerly, no difficulty arose upon this point. Although, by a few, the term was understood not of actual days, but figuratively, still, as the real antiquity of the earth was not suspected, no one who accepted the general teaching of Christian theology found any difficulty in believing that the visible universe was created by the Almighty in six literal days, about 4000 years before the birth of Christ.[1] But knowledge has advanced, and this position is no longer tenable. Geology has become a science, and has disclosed to us, upon evidence which cannot be gainsaid, the immeasurable antiquity of our globe, the great physical changes which its surface has undergone, the innumerable multitude of living forms by which in ascending progression, from the lowly marine organisms which mark the dawn of life, it has been successively peopled. Those white cliffs which tower out of the sea in many parts of our southern coasts are built up from the shells of minute

[1] See, for instance, the passage quoted above, p. 37.

creatures, deposited, at the rate of a few inches a century, at the bottom of the ocean, and afterwards by some mighty upheaval of the earth's crust raised aloft above the waves. Our coal measures are the remains of mighty forests, astir with a multitudinous insect life, which through untold centuries have come and gone, storing up the energy poured forth by the sun for our consumption and enjoyment. These are but two of the many instances which might be given, demonstrating the immense antiquity of our globe. Our earth bears within itself the marks of a past history reaching back to an age incalculably anterior to that at which man first appeared upon it. If now the term *day* is to be understood literally, it is clear that the narrative of Genesis cannot accord with the teaching of geology: are we at liberty, then, to understand it in any other way?

This question must be answered, not by a discussion as to the proper meaning of the Hebrew term employed (respecting which there is no doubt), but by inquiring whether or not it may have been used by the writer metaphorically. Although there are no precise parallels in the Old Testament for such a metaphorical use of the word, it seems, on the whole, reasonable to concede it here. The author, it may be supposed, while conscious that the Divine operation could not be measured by human standards of time, nevertheless was desirous of accommodating artificially the period of creation to the divisions of the week; and hence adopted the term *day* in a

THE FIRST CHAPTER OF GENESIS. 167

figurative sense. If this view be correct, the term will have been used by him consciously, as a metaphor, for the purpose of his representation, it being really his intention to designate by it a period of time. The several "days," with their "mornings" and "evenings," will thus be the form under which the work is represented as taking place; they will not constitute part of the reality.[1] When, however, it has been granted, as at least a possible interpretation, that the "days" may represent periods, has the required end been attained? Does the order in which the different parts of the visible universe were produced, as stated in the narrative of Genesis, accord with the order which is taught by science? The answer, though it may cause surprise to some, must be given explicitly and frankly. They do *not* accord. Not only do they not accord, but the disagreements are of a nature which it is hazardous and precarious to count upon future discovery removing. Even if we shrink from affirming that they *cannot* so be removed, we must admit that they are of a character which makes it prudent not to rely upon such a contingency. Practically, in other words, we must reckon with them now. It will be sufficient if I point out briefly the two principal discrepancies. According to the Book of Genesis, the earth was clothed with vegetation two days, or periods, before animal life appeared upon it. According to the evidence of the rocks, plant life, from the beginning, in its earliest and humblest forms, was

[1] See Note A (p. 177).

accompanied by similar humble types of animal life: and the two advanced gradually together, side by side, till the higher and more complete types of each were attained. Secondly, the formation of the heavenly bodies not merely after the creation of the earth, but after the appearance upon it of vegetation, is inconsistent with the entire conception of the solar system as revealed by science, not less than with the process by which that system itself is supposed to have come into being. Both the stars in their far-distant courses, and the planetary system with which this globe is more immediately connected, form a vast and wonderfully constituted order, so marked by correlation of structure and unity of design as to forbid the supposition that a particular body, such as this earth, was created prior to the whole of which it is a single and subordinate part. Nor is this all. The commonly accepted theory of the formation of the solar system does not permit the consolidation of the earth, and the appearance upon it of seas and vegetation at a time while the substance of which the sun was composed was still in a diffused state. Not to enter here into further details, the conclusion, whether we will it or not, is forced upon us that both geology and astronomy directly contradict the narrative of Genesis.[1]

In face of these discrepancies (which are not all that might be mentioned), what attitude are we to assume? Are we, with one class of thinkers, to con-

[1] See Note B (p. 177).

THE FIRST CHAPTER OF GENESIS. 169

clude that their presence is fatal to the entire revelation of which apparently they form part? This would be a hasty and ill-considered conclusion. Or are we to imitate others, and, doing violence now to the testimony of science, now to the express words of Genesis, to seek to reconcile what—however reluctantly we may make the admission—is irreconcilable? We embark then upon an enterprise doomed to failure. Or is the presence of these discrepancies an indication that we must modify our conception of the scope of the narrative, and consider whether we have not misapprehended its true purport; whether its true purport is not to be sought in a different direction altogether from that which we had imagined? It is difficult not to think that the last is the wise and right alternative to adopt. These very discrepancies are an indication that the real object of the narrative in Genesis is not to teach *scientific* truth, but to teach *religious* truth. If this, its true purport, be kept in view, it will be seen neither to come into collision with science, nor to need reconciliation with it. It moves in a different plane altogether. From this point of view, as we shall see, its teaching has an independent value of its own, and can never become antiquated or obsolete. Let me indicate, in its main features, what this teaching is.

One object of the narrative will be evident at once: it is to show, in opposition to the crude conceptions current in many parts of the ancient world, that the world is not self-originated; that it was called into existence, and brought gradually into its present state, at the will of a Spiritual Being, prior to it, independent of it, deliberately planning each stage of its development. The dignified and sublime representation which it gives is in marked contrast to the self-contradictory, grotesque speculations which form the usual staple of the ancient cosmogonies. This feature is to be the more insisted on, because it is the one which distinguishes it essentially from that Chaldæan account of the Creation, recovered a few years ago from the ruins of Nineveh, with which it has been sometimes compared.[1] There exists indeed a similarity of outline, sufficient to suggest the inference that in their broader features both may be derived from some common source : but here the resemblance ends. In other respects the Babylonian scheme is entirely polytheistic : chaos is anterior to deity ; and as the earth gradually assumes shape, the gods of the Assyrian pantheon emerge at the same time from the surging deep.[2] How different is the representation in Genesis! The absolute supremacy of the Deity, His power to mould and dispose all things to His own purpose, the perfect realization

[1] The Chaldæan account may be read in Schrader's *Cuneiform Inscriptions and the Old Testament* (1883), on Gen. i. 1, 14, 20 ; or in *Records of the Past*, second series, i. (1888) p. 133 ff. (in a different version, p. 149 ff.).

[2] See lines 7-12 of the first tablet (Schrader, p. 2 ; *Records of the Past*, p. 133). The two translations differ in some details, but not substantially. That of Schrader forms the basis of the extract in the *Expositor*, Jan. 1886, p. 39.

of His design, marking the entire work, and noted by the recurring formula, "And God saw that it was good," could not be more distinctly or more emphatically expressed. It is the record of the unique relation in which every part of the world stands to its Maker, a relation in which (as the usage of the word rendered *create* appears to imply [1]) it stands to none besides. The *fact* of a creator is the fundamental teaching of the cosmogony of Genesis: to that fact it was a witness in the ancient world, in times when it was ill-apprehended or obscured, and to that fact it is a witness still. For the fact is one, it should be recollected, which no scientific progress can affect or disprove: science may instruct us indefinitely in the hidden processes of Nature; theology tells us what science, as such, cannot tell us, that these processes are not ultimate, that they are arranged and ordered by a Divine Mind. Much confusion and controversy would be avoided, could this distinction be firmly apprehended. Rightly understood, science and theology are not antagonistic, but *supplementary*. Science discloses merely the mechanical and physical processes of which the course of nature consists: except when it passes beyond its province, it affirms nothing —but it also denies nothing—respecting that invisible Power by which, as we believe, they have been concerted and regulated. Here, then, is one characteristic feature in the teaching of the first chapter of Genesis.

Secondly, we must conclude, the chapter is not

[1] See Note C (p. 178).

meant to teach *authoritatively* the actual past history of the earth. It is not a revelation of what may be discoverable by natural methods; and it is mistaking its purport altogether either, on the one hand, to hold it up as contradicting modern scientific discoveries, or on the other, to repeat the well-intentioned, but vain, endeavour to reconcile it with them. Its object is to afford a view true in conception, if not in detail, of the origin of the earth as we know it, and to embody this not in an abstract or confused form which may soon be forgotten, but in a series of *representative pictures* which may impress themselves upon the imagination, and in each one of which the truth is insisted on, that the stage which it represents is no product of chance, or of mere mechanical forces, but that it is an act of the Divine will. It teaches, in terms which all can understand, the same truth which is the outcome of the wisest philosophy, that the world in which we live, and have our being, cannot be comprehended, cannot be an intelligible object of knowledge, except as dependent on a supreme Mind. With this view it divides artificially the periods of the earth's formation. It groups the living creatures upon its surface under the great subdivisions which appeal to the eye, and declares each to have been produced in accordance with the Divine Will, each to owe its being to the Divine intention. It states the fact of their creation: it is silent on the secondary causes through which, in particular cases, or even more generally, they may have been developed. Within the two great groups of vegetable and animal life it imposes no veto on the action of natural causes in the production of species. Their production by the persistent accumulation of minute variations may or may not be true scientifically—upon that question I have no right to pronounce an opinion—but, in so far as it is true, it involves no derogation from the supremacy of the Creator, no denial of His ever-present operation and providence. The doctrine of the gradual formation of species will be but the exhibition in detail of those processes which the writer of this chapter of Genesis sums up into a single phrase, and apparently compresses into a single moment, for the purpose of declaring their dependence on the Divine Will. A third point on which the record insists is the distinctive pre-eminence belonging to man. "Let us make man in our image, after our likeness." Let us not deceive ourselves. The structural similarity between man and some of the higher animals is no conclusive proof that he does not possess powers differing in kind, and not in degree only, from theirs. A true estimate of human nature will take account of it as a whole; it will not view it from its lower side alone. What, then, do we suppose to be meant when it is said that man was made in the "image of God"? It is meant that he has been endowed with that highest and noblest of gifts, the gift of *self-conscious reason.* In all that is implied by this: in the various intellectual faculties possessed by him; in that creative and originative power, which we all possess in greater or less degree, but which is the pre-eminent characteristic of genius; in the power of rising superior to the impulses of sense, of subduing and transforming them, and, while we know both, of choosing the good and refusing the evil; in the ability to pass beyond ourselves, and enter into new relations with our fellowmen, relations of sympathy, affection, compassion, and love; in that capacity for a *character*, with which our happiness is so strangely linked; in the power, lastly, of knowing and loving God partially here, as we hope to know and love Him more completely hereafter — is not man in all these respects an adumbration, however faint, a reflex, however dimmed by obscuring shadows, of the supreme perfection of the Creator? Are not these the features in which he differs, and differs essentially, from the beasts that perish? Are they not those in virtue of which God can make Himself known to him, can reveal to him His purposes of grace, and grant him the promise of eternal life?

Such are some of the chief theological doctrines implied in the Cosmogony of Genesis. It teaches the absolute supremacy of the Creator in His work of Creation: it exhibits to us, in a series of *representative pictures*, how every stage of His work was dependent upon His will and realized His purpose: it emphasizes the distinctive pre-eminence belonging to man. These are theological truths, not truths of science.[1]

[1] See Note D (p. 178).

THE FIRST CHAPTER OF GENESIS. 175

It is imperative that the Christian teacher should distinguish what can, and what cannot, be claimed for the narrative of Genesis. He should not wait for the admission to be extorted from him by an opponent: he should be beforehand himself with a theory, which, recognizing alike the claims of theology and science, will be just to each, and render each its due. The interpretation of the first chapter of Genesis has never been fixed by the Church, and forms no article in the Christian Creed. It is the duty of the Christian teacher, on the one hand, to state frankly that such discrepancies as have been alluded to exist, and on the other to point out that their recognition is no derogation to the Christian revelation, and in no respect imperils the Christian faith. There are many minds acute enough to perceive the truth of the first of these propositions, but not able with equal clearness to discern the truth of the second. The unreality of the reconciliations sometimes proposed by commentators is detected at once by those who are at the pains to examine the subject for themselves. Above all things, it is the duty of those at the present day who see more clearly to express themselves in terms which cannot be misunderstood.[1]

But to return in conclusion for a few moments to the words with which I began. " Where wast thou when I laid the foundations of the world ?" Science studied rightly, promotes, not the pride of intellect,

[1] See Note E (p. 178).

but humility. Year by year, as fresh conquests are gained, now in some remote corner of the universe, now in the structure of some minute organism scarcely visible to the eye, we acquire new and unexpected insight into the operations of Divine Wisdom; we are impressed more and more with the magnitude and profundity of the design which is stamped upon the physical creation. But Job's answer to the question put to him must also be ours. We may follow back in imagination, to their earliest beginnings, the long succession of living forms which have peopled our earth, we may infer somewhat respecting the gigantic movements which took place when the foundations of this world were being laid; but when we have gone thus far, a vaster unknown than Job could even imagine looms through the darkness beyond. In whatever direction we turn our eye, it can descry no traces of an end: on the contrary, it discovers more and more which we cannot account for or explain. After twenty-five centuries, as we survey the physical universe, we must confess with Job himself, in another place: "Lo, these are but the outskirts of his ways," and "the whisper of a word" is still all that "we hear of him."[1]

[1] Job xxvi. 14.

ADDITIONAL NOTES TO SERMON VIII.

NOTE A.

It must be admitted, however, that this interpretation of "day" is uncertain, and that the distinction which is regularly made between "evening" and "morning" is opposed to it. There is force also in Dr. Ladd's remarks: "It would be a mistake to suppose that *six entire days* are taken for creation because God needs time in order that His will and wisdom may reach their result. To the Hebrew mind the majesty of Jehovah consists in His having His will done without any intervening time. Of the long geological periods, and slow, involved processes, and patient, everlasting evolution of results by building one stage upon the preceding stage, which modern physical science emphasizes, the Hebrew mind had not the least conception as a necessity or fact of creation. It is divine to speak, and have the word at once accomplished [Ps. xxxiii. 9]. The six days of creation are none of them to be regarded as in any sense *filled up* with the Divine work. To think of Jehovah as engaged all day in getting accomplished the task appropriate to each period would doubtless have seemed to the sacred writer degrading to His majesty" (*What is the Bible?* New York, 1890, p. 137 f.).

NOTE B.

For the grounds of the statements contained in this paragraph, the writer may be permitted to refer to an article on "The Cosmogony of Genesis," contributed by him to the *Expositor*, Jan. 1886, pp. 23-45, where also some account is given of the principal schemes of reconciliation which have been proposed.

On the violent methods of interpretation by which the eminent geologist, Prof. Dana, thinks it possible to harmonize the narrative of Genesis with the teachings of science, see the *Andover* (U. S. A.) *Review*, Dec., 1887, p. 641 ff. It surely is not legitimate or reasonable, for instance, to understand "earth" and "waters" in Gen. i. 2 as denoting nothing resembling what these words ordinarily signify in Hebrew, but matter in that unimaginable condition when it was not yet endowed with force, and the power of molecular action ; or to suppose that "waters" in Gen. i. 6 is a term descriptive of the attenuated substance of the universe while yet diffused, in a nebulous or vaporous form, through space.

Note C.

The word means properly, as it seems, *to cut* or *shape* (in the intensive conjugation, it is used in Josh. xvii. 17 of cutting down trees ; and in Phœnician—see the *Corpus Inscriptionum Semiticarum*, Tom. i. No. 347—it denotes the employment of some kind of artificer) ; but in the simple conjugation it is used in the Old Testament exclusively of God.

Note D.

Human nature, as a whole, becomes the subject-matter of *science*, only in so far as the functions of the brain are treated as *exclusively* physiological. This treatment of them will not however be conceded by philosophy to include the whole truth. Consciousness is *conditioned*—so far as our experience enables us to judge—by a physical organism, but cannot be resolved into a *mere* function of it.

Note E.

Very just views on the nature and purpose of the Biblical narrative are to be found in Dr. Ladd's volume, quoted in Note A, chap. v., p. 126 ff.

SERMON IX.[1]

THE WARRIOR FROM EDOM.

Is. lxiii. 1 : " Who is this that cometh from Edom, with dyed garments from Bozrah? this that is glorious in his apparel, travelling in the greatness of his strength ?"

THE first six verses of the portion of the Book of Isaiah appointed to be read for the Epistle in this morning's service, constitute a whole, distinguished alike in subject and in tone from the part which follows. The imaginative power, which in the great prophecy beginning with the fortieth chapter, and extending to the end of the book, so often kindles our admiration, has produced in these few verses one of its most striking creations. Let us study it to-night with a view of ascertaining its import and significance. The last twenty-seven chapters of the Book of Isaiah were designed primarily for the reassurance and encouragement of the Jewish exiles, who, after the city and temple had been captured by the troops of Nebuchadnezzar, were removed in a body to Babylon. That this is the situation of those whom

[1] Preached in the Cathedral, on the evening of Monday in Holy Week, 1884.

the prophet is addressing, is apparent from many indications—amongst others from the words occurring in the chapter which next follows, descriptive of that same terrible and overwhelming disaster, to the pathetic description of which we have been listening in the First Lesson this evening :—" Thy holy cities are become a wilderness; Zion is become a wilderness, Jerusalem a desolation. Our holy and beautiful house, where our fathers praised thee, is burned with fire; and all our pleasant things are laid waste." [1] The captivity in Babylon lasted for long : Jeremiah had warned the exiles that they must look for no speedy return ; he had bidden them build houses and plant vineyards in their foreign home ; [2] for, from the date of Nebuchadnezzar's first conquests, seventy years, he declared, would elapse before the banished people were restored.[3] The exiles, it would seem, obeyed Jeremiah's directions : the life, at first so strange, grew familiar to them, so that among their children, in the next generation, there were many content with the conditions in which they found themselves, and in no way eager for a change. Thus, when the promised limit drew nigh, and the deliverer, Cyrus, appeared in the distance, there were some who viewed the prospect of a return to their ancient country with unconcern; while others, whose temper

---

[1] Is. lxiv. 10-11. Cf. Lam. ii. 13-22.

[2] Jer. xxviii., xxix. 4-10.

[3] Jer. xxv. 11 f. (belonging to the year in which Nebuchadnezzar defeated the troops of Pharaoh Necho at Carchemish, B.C. 604).

was different, were despondent or incredulous, not believing that the promised deliverance would be effected.[1] On the return of the nation to Judæa great issues, indeed, were staked : but the mass of the people did not, perhaps could not, realize what they were ; and the Babylonian monarchy seemed to be so firmly established, that it was deemed doubtful if any power could break its strength. To overcome such indifference and want of faith is the main scope of this group of chapters; and the prophet elaborates his theme with unrivalled dramatic and rhetorical force. Again and again, each time under a new and telling figure, he assures his people that their God, who presides over nature, and directs the movements of history, will so shape its course now, that Israel's release will be effected, and the nation be thus enabled to complete its future destiny. Its enemies will be powerless, their efforts foiled : " no weapon," he exclaims, "that is formed against thee shall prosper."[2]

This now is the thought which, with singular grandeur of conception, is set before us in the short section which I ask you to consider with me to-night. Let me first explain briefly the details.

> Who is this that cometh from Edom,
> With dyed garments from Bozrah ?
> This that is glorious in his apparel,
> Marching in the greatness of his strength ?

---

[1] Comp. Is. xl. 27, xlvi. 12 (the "stout-hearted," who refuse to credit the prophet's announcement), xlix. 14.

[2] xli. 15 f., xlix. 25 f., l. 22 f., liv. 17, &c.

SERMON IX.

The prophet sees a figure, as of a Conqueror, with crimsoned garments, advancing, proudly and majestically, from the direction of Edom. The Edomites were old and embittered enemies of Israel; and the writings of the prophets contain many allusions to the rivalry and unfriendly feeling subsisting between the two nations.[1] In particular, we learn from Ezekiel that they had evinced special delight on the occasion when Jerusalem was captured by the Chaldæans, which seemed to them a proof that the Chosen People were no better than the heathen.[2] The appearance of the Conqueror from Edom, then, implies that one of Israel's most inveterate foes has been humiliated. The prophet, affecting ignorance, inquires who he is: he hears in reply the words—

I that speak in righteousness, mighty to save,

or, as we might paraphrase, I who have announced a just and righteous purpose of deliverance,[3] and am able to give it effect. The answer does not satisfy the inquirer: it does not explain the crimsoned

[1] Amos i. 11, Jer. xlix. 12, Ob. 10-16, Lam. iv. 21 f., Ezek. xxxv. 5 (a "perpetual enmity"), Is. xxxiv., Joel iii. 19, Mal. i. 2-4.

[2] Ezek. xxxv. 5 ("Because thou hast had a perpetual enmity, and hast given over the children of Israel to the power of the sword in the day of their calamity"), 10 ("Because thou hast said, These two nations and these two countries shall be mine, and we will possess it"), 12 ("I the LORD have heard all thy blasphemies which thou hast spoken against the mountains of Israel, saying, They are laid desolate, they are given us to devour"). Comp. Ezek. xxv. 12, Ps. cxxxvii. 7, and Is. xxxiv. 8 (the "quarrel of Zion," viz. with Edom).

[3] Comp. for the expression xlv. 19.

garments which first attracted his attention. The prophet, therefore, asks again more directly—

> Wherefore art thou red in thine apparel,
> And thy garments like him that treadeth the wine-press?

The answer follows—

> The wine-press I have trodden alone;
> And of the peoples, no man was with me:

among all the nations of the earth, no one assisted Him—

> And I have trodden them in mine anger, and trampled them in my fury;
> And their life-stream is sprinkled upon my garments,
> And I have stained all my raiment.

Not Edom only, but the other nations as well, hostile to God and to His people, have been trodden down and subdued—

> For the day of vengeance was in my heart;
> And the year of my redeemed was come:

the time had arrived for My people to be delivered, and My purpose was one of vengeance on their foes.

> And I looked, but there was none to help.
> And I was amazed that there was none to uphold:
> Therefore mine own arm brought salvation to me;
> And my fury, it upheld me.

No one, the meaning is, willingly and consciously offered to help forward the work: nevertheless, God's purpose accomplished itself, human means, in so far as they were used by Him, being His instruments unconsciously.

> And I trod down the peoples in mine anger,
> And brake them in pieces in my fury,
> And I brought down their life-stream to the earth.

SERMON IX.

At this point the subject changes ; and in the rest of the chapter, as in chapter lxiv., the prophet no longer questions Jehovah in dialogue, he addresses Jehovah as a suppliant, speaking in his people's name, and entreating Him for a renewal of the mercies shown to Israel in the past.

It is obvious that the expressions used in this passage are not to be interpreted literally. They do not describe any event in history, as it actually occurred. The prophets seize the great principles of God's government of the world, and set them forth in a symbolical, or imaginative, dress ; and we must penetrate through this symbolism of form, if we wish to discover the fundamental truth, or truths, to which it gives expression.[1] Here it is plain that the fundamental thought is the impotence of the nations to arrest God's purposes at a critical moment in the history of His people. That is the truth which was of immediate, practical interest to the prophet. It is the truth which, as I have remarked before, it is his aim effectually to bring home to his readers, and by which he seeks to encourage and re-assure them in face of the obstacles which at least many amongst them imagined to beset their nation's future. And it is manifest how much more impressive the prophet's representation is, how much better adapted to secure the end desired, than an abstract verbal enunciation would have been. It is one of those applications of figurative language, the product of the imaginative

[1] Cf. above, p. 108.

faculty, which the higher style of human composition is always ready to employ, which appealed with peculiar force to an Eastern people, and which recur, under one form or another, in many different parts of the Bible.

In what connexion, however, does the passage stand with the events which we commemorate at this sacred season? It is not possible to understand it as referring directly to the passion or triumph of our Blessed Lord: in the prophecy, the conqueror is bestained not with his own blood, but with that of his victims, and his enemies are not spiritual foes, but the nations of the world. The language is too express to leave any doubt on this point. But though not a direct prediction of the Agony of Christ, it may be brought very naturally into connexion with it. We may regard it as a type, or emblematic representation, of that triumph of God over the enemies opposed to Him, which is re-enacted again and again in the course of history, but which in its completest form, and with far-reaching results, was accomplished in the Passion and Death of our Blessed Lord. In itself, it was designed as an encouragement to the Jewish exiles in Babylon, showing them, by a signal example, how the most determined opposition to the welfare of God's people would be overcome; but this opposition, as we know both from history and from individual experience, has not been confined to one occasion only; it is repeated in history, under many different circumstances, and in many different forms. And the greatest triumph achieved over it, was the triumph gained by Christ. Our Church, then, to-day directs our thoughts to the grand conception drawn by the prophet's inspired imagination: and though every detail does not correspond with exactness, bids us see in it a type, or figure, of that greater conflict, in which the enemies overcome were not the nations of the earth, but the powers of darkness, and of which the issue was not the temporal restoration of the Chosen People, but the restitution from spiritual bondage of fallen humanity. The truth that man's opposition cannot thwart God's saving purposes, that He will, if need be, carry them through unaided, is signally and wonderfully exemplified in the closing events of our Lord's life upon earth. The Warrior in the prophecy is a Divine One, just as the Victor in the New Testament is the God-man. Certainly to the outward eye, His course during that last week seemed to be one of humiliation and reverse, the blood with which His garments were stained was His own life-blood, and death, not victory, seemed to be the close. But in the spiritual conflict, the Passion was itself a triumph; and the blood was the symbol not of defeat, but of victory. The Passion and Death of Christ brought to nought him that had the power of death, and inaugurated the "year of" Jehovah's "redeemed." And this is the point of view from which the Cross is alluded to by the Apostle. In his Epistle to the Colossians, St. Paul says that Christ, "having stripped off from himself the principalities and the powers," *i.e.* having released Himself from the evil assailants which clung round Him and strove to bring Him down, "made a show of them openly, triumphing over them upon it."[1] The Cross, that is, is regarded ideally by the Apostle as the scene of a triumph, the triumph of Christ, the Head and representative of humanity, over the power of sin and evil.

There is, however, in the New Testament an allusion to the prophecy which we have been considering, which deserves to be noticed in the present connexion. The seer of the Apocalypse, in one of his later visions, sees one having the name of the Word of God, clad, like the warrior of the prophet, with a vesture sprinkled in blood, who smites the nations with a sharp sword, and treads the winepress of the fierce wrath of Almighty God.[2] Dark and mysterious as the Apocalypse must always largely remain, it seems at least to be clear that what is contemplated in this vision is the final consummation of that which is at present only inchoate, the subjugation of sin and evil, when Christ shall have put all things under His feet, and judgment shall have been finally executed upon His enemies. The Divine warrior, as before, accomplishes His work alone: and He treads the wine-press, as the agent of God's wrath, against the representatives of sin and evil. It is the completion, as a fact, of the work already completed potentially upon Golgotha.

[1] Col. ii. 15.   [2] Rev. xix. 13-16.

But let us return to the passage with which we started. A comment on the spirit in which we should read it is afforded by the passage which immediately follows.[1] There the prophet addresses Jehovah in his people's name; and in the assured conviction that the redemption, guaranteed by His triumph, will be accomplished, supplies faithful Israel with a hymn of thanksgiving, supplication, and confession, expressive of the frame of mind worthy to receive it. In words of surpassing eloquence and beauty, he celebrates the lovingkindnesses of the Lord, and the great goodness bestowed by Him upon the house of Israel, recalling how in His love and in His pity He redeemed them in the days of old from Egypt, and how afterwards they had rebelled and vexed His Holy Spirit, until He was turned to be their enemy, and fought against them. Then follows the appeal, heard in this section for the first and only time in the Old Testament, to the Fatherhood of God,—" Doubtless thou art our Father, though Abraham be ignorant of us, and Israel acknowledge us not; thou, O LORD, art our father; our redeemer from of old is thy name. O LORD, why dost thou cause us to err from thy ways, and hardenest our heart from thy fear? Return for thy servants' sake, the tribes of thy inheritance." The pure and intense emotion with which the prophet contemplates the benefits conferred upon his people, the confession of their own unworthiness, his faith in God's fatherly care for His people, and the assurance

[1] Is. lxiii. 7—lxiv. 12.

with which he looks forward to the promised restoration, are models of the attitude of mind which we also may make our own, and in which we may in particular meditate on the deliverance effected for us by the sufferings of Christ. Benefits and mercies greater than those of which Israel partook have been bestowed upon us: let us bear in thankful remembrance the sufferings and the triumph, not our own, which secured them for us. Let us fix our eyes in devout contemplation on the events which day by day at this season are set before us ; and endeavour, by God's help, in the spirit which the prophet has taught us, to receive and to use worthily the blessings derived therefrom, of which we have been made the inheritors.

SERMON X.[1]

THE SIXTY-EIGHTH PSALM.

Ps. lxviii. 18 : " Thou hast ascended on high, thou hast led (thy) captivity captive; thou hast received gifts among men, yea, among the rebellious also, that the LORD God might dwell (there)."

THESE words form part of the Psalm, the sixty-eighth, which we have heard in this morning's service. The period of history to which the Psalm belongs is uncertain ; some parts wear the appearance of being ancient, others present features which point with some cogency towards a later date. The Old Testament affords many examples of a writer incorporating, and adapting to his own use, phrases, and even entire verses, originally written, on an altogether different occasion, by another hand ;[2] and it is possible that this is the solution of the phænomena which the Psalm presents. Certainly, two verses are quoted,

---

[1] Preached in the Cathedral on Sunday, Nov. 13, 1887.

[2] Comp. for example, Is. ii. 2-4 with Mic. iv. 1-3 ; Jer. xlviii. with Is. xv.-xvi. (see the margin of the former, in the Revised Version); Jer. xlix. 9-10, 14-16 with Obad. 5-6, 1-4 ; Is. xxiv. 17-18 with Jer. xlviii. 43-44 ; Ps. xcvi. 7, 8ª, 9ª with Ps. xxix. 1-2 ; Ps. xcviii. 1ª, 3ᵇ with Is. xlii. 10, lii. 10, &c. (In some of the instances the phraseology is slightly varied.)

nearly word for word, from the Song of Deborah, in the fifth chapter of the Book of Judges [1]; and this being so, it is quite conceivable that other verses may be quoted from some earlier sources extant at the time when the Psalm was composed, but now lost. When we read in the fourth verse—not, "Magnify him that rideth upon the heavens as it were upon an horse," but, as we ought to read, and as in the Revised Version we do read, "Cast up a highway for him that rideth through the deserts," we are reminded involuntarily of the words in which the prophet bids a path be made ready in the wilderness, for the people soon to be restored from its exile in Babylon—" In the wilderness prepare ye the way of the LORD; make straight in the desert a highway for our God." [2] This verse is the only parallel to the one in the Psalm which the Old Testament affords: and the similarity is so striking that we can hardly be wrong, especially when we find it confirmed by other indications, in being guided by it in fixing a date for the Psalm. The Psalm will in any case not be earlier than the closing years of the Babylonian captivity; and it is a reasonable conjecture that it was written in view of the approaching return of the exiled nation to Palestine, and of God's re-entry into His ancient sanctuary on Zion. The Psalmist views the coming deliverance as a great manifestation

[1] Ps. lxviii. 7-8; comp. Jud. v. 4-5.
[2] Is. xl. 3 : comp. lvii. 14, lxii. 10, where the same expression *cast up a way*—viz. for the returning nation—is used.

of Jehovah's power, and a triumph over Israel's foes: and so he opens in tones of hope and exultation, almost quoting the words of the old war-cry, which was used when the Ark was moved—[1]

> Let God arise, let his enemies be scattered,
> And let them that hate him flee before him.

Throughout the Psalm is pitched in the same triumphant key: it is the most buoyant, the most animated, the most powerful which is to be found in the Psalter. At least, the only Psalm which could contest with it this description would be that other not less noble one, the eighteenth. His jubilant exordium ended, the Psalmist turns to review the former history of his nation. The prospect of the immediate return to Palestine kindles his imagination, and animates his pen: under vivid and impressive figures he describes the journey of Israel through the wilderness, and its triumphant occupation of the land of Canaan, culminating in the choice of Zion as the abode of God, and His solemn entry into it; for he sees in these glories of the past a type, or pledge, of the people's speedy deliverance now, and of their restoration to their ancient home. In this review of the

---

[1] Num. x. 35. The change of "Jehovah" to "God" is due, in all probability, not to the author of the Psalm, but to the collector who compiled Book II. of the Psalms (Ps. xlii.-lxxii.), and who, like the compiler of Ps. lxxiii.-lxxxiii., sought to avoid, as far as possible, the use of the former term, replacing it usually by the latter (comp. especially Ps. liii. with Ps. xiv., and Ps. lxx. with Ps. xl. 13-17). See Prof. Kirkpatrick's *The Psalms* (*Book I.*), pp. xli, xlii; or the writer's *Introduction*, pp. 349-351.

THE SIXTY-EIGHTH PSALM. 193

past, the Song of Deborah is the clue to the Psalmist's thought. Quoting from it, almost verbally, he first notices the departure from Sinai—

> O God, when thou wentest forth before thy people,
> When thou marchedst through the wilderness,
> The earth trembled, the heavens also dropped before God,
> Yon Sinai trembled at the presence of God, the God of Israel.[1]

Passing on, he recalls the memory of the gifts and benefits with which God visited His people in the wilderness—

> A bounteous rain, O God, thou didst shower down:
> When thine inheritance was weary, *thou* didst confirm it.

Next he glances at the successes won by Israel, during its early occupation of Palestine: no sooner was the signal, or command, uttered, than victory followed immediately, and the maidens [2] of Israel flocked forth to greet the victor and proclaim the news—

> The Lord gave the word:
> The women that brought the tidings were a great host.

He quotes fragments from an ancient battle-song, sung by the women on such an occasion—

> Kings of armies do flee, do flee:
> And she that tarrieth at home divideth the spoil.

He passes to narrate the choice of Zion, after David's conquest of it from the Jebusites, as the abode of God, and His solemn entry into it. Here, first of all,

---
[1] Comp. Jud. v. 4-5.
[2] Comp. 1 Sam. xviii. 7 ; 2 Sam. i. 20 (daughters).

he poetically imagines other mountains, especially the huge and massive range of Bashan, on the east of Jordan, as viewing with ill-disguised envy the honour bestowed upon the comparatively insignificant hill of Zion, and claiming to be not less worthy of it themselves—

> A mountain of God[1] is the mountain of Bashan;
> A mountain of many heights is the mountain of Bashan.
> Why look ye askance, ye mountains of many heights,
> At the mountain which God hath desired for his abode?
> Yea, Jehovah will dwell in it for ever.

Next, he describes, under figures borrowed from the triumph of an earthly conqueror, God's entry into the abode thus chosen for Himself: at the head of armies of angels He enters the sanctuary on Zion—

> The chariots of God are twenty thousand, even thousands redoubled:
> The Lord is come from[2] Sinai into the sanctuary.
> Thou hast ascended on high,
> Thou hast led (thy) captivity captive;
> Thou hast received gifts among men,
> Yea, among the refractory also, that Jah God might dwell (there).

The Psalmist pictures to himself a triumphal procession, winding up the newly-conquered hill of Zion, the figure being that of a victor, taking possession of

---

[1] *I.e.* a mountain worthy of God, a noble mountain.

[2] The Hebrew text has "is among them," which in connexion with what follows yields such an imperfect sense that it is necessary to suppose an error in the reading. The correction here adopted only involves the addition of a single letter (בא מסיני for בם סיני), and has been approved by Nowack, Cheyne, and others. Similarly also Bishop Perowne.

the enemy's citadel, and with his train of captives and spoil following him in the triumph. One of the phrases, here used, is sometimes misunderstood. The expression "led captivity captive" is sometimes taken to mean, "led captive and subdued the power which enthralled others," the word "captivity" being almost personified. But in fact, *captivity* is simply an abstract term denoting *captives*, as is at once shown by the passage from the Song of Deborah, from which the expression here used is evidently borrowed [1]—"Arise, Barak, *and lead thy captivity captive*, thou son of Abinoam." Thus the phrase just means, "Hast led in triumph the captives which thou hast taken." In the words following, "*Hast received gifts among men*," the Psalmist alludes to the tribute offered either by the vanquished foes themselves, or by others who come forward spontaneously to own the victor, and secure his favour. And, he adds, even those who have held out most obstinately, even the stubborn or refractory ones, are now ready to offer homage, that "Jah God may dwell (there)," in the home which He has chosen, with none to dispute His possession of it. Here the climax of the Psalm is reached. David's occupation of Jerusalem and the entry of God into the Tent prepared for Him there,[2] are the pledge and symbol of the coming re-occupation of the Holy City, and the re-entry of God into the Temple soon to be restored. Hence in the rest of

---

[1] Jud. v. 12.
[2] 2 Sam. vi. 17; cf. vii. 2.

the Psalm, the Psalmist leaves the past, and contemplates exclusively the present or the future. He calls upon Israel to praise God as their Benefactor and Deliverer, and as the God who has promised them vengeance upon their enemies.[1] Next he draws an ideal picture of the festal processions with which, before long, the Temple will be re-dedicated,—Zebulun and Naphtali, the two tribes which Deborah had singled out for special honour in her Song, being named as representing the ten tribes, whom he views, like the prophets,[2] as sharing ideally in the restoration. Lastly, also in agreement with the prophets, he anticipates the day when, Jehovah having shown Himself "strong" for Israel, and "scattered the peoples who delight in war," the nations of the earth will acknowledge Israel's religion, and render homage to the God whose throne is on Zion—

> Command [3] thy strength, O God;
> Show thyself strong, O God, thou who hast wrought for
>   us [4] out of thy temple.
> Unto Jerusalem shall kings bring presents unto thee.

He mentions, in particular, as Isaiah had done before

---

[1] *Vv.* 19-23.

[2] *E.g.* Hos. iii. 5, Jer. iii. 18, xxvi. 4-6, 18-20, Ezek. xxxvii. 15 ff., xlviii. 1 ff. See a different explanation in Cheyne's note *ad loc.*

[3] So, with a change of punctuation, many ancient versions and modern commentators. מהיכלך in *v.* 29 (Heb. 30) is difficult. The rendering "Because of thy temple" being not very natural, it is easiest, perhaps, to connect the word with the preceding verse (so R. V. *marg.*): for the idea, cf. xiv. 7ª, xx. 3, cxxviii. 5. With "to work for," comp. Is. lxiv. 4 (Heb. 3).

[4] *Viz.* in the past: the perfect tense as Ps. xxxi. 19, xl. 5, &c.

him,[1] Egypt and Ethiopia, as examples of powerful and wealthy nations, hastening forward with tokens of allegiance—

> Princes shall come out of Egypt,
> Ethiopia shall hasten to stretch forth her hands unto God.

And he closes with a summons, addressed not to Israel only, but to "all the kingdoms of the earth," to honour duly God, who is throned on high in the heavens, but who manifests Himself also with power upon earth as the Protector and Redeemer of His people—

> Ascribe ye strength unto God:
> Whose majesty is over Israel, and his strength is in the skies.
> O God, thou art terrible out of thy holy places:
> The God of Israel, he giveth strength and power unto the people.
> Blessed be God.

The verse which I have taken for my text is quoted by St. Paul in his Epistle to the Ephesians, in a somewhat different form. Speaking of the various gifts conferred upon members of the Church, he writes,[2] "But unto each one of us was the grace given according to the measure of the gift of Christ. Wherefore he saith, When he ascended on high, he led captivity captive, and gave gifts unto men." St. Paul is not here following the genuine text of the Psalm, but is in all probability guided by an old Jewish interpretation with which he was familiar, and

---

[1] Is. xviii. 7, xix. 18-25. [2] Eph. iv. 7-8.

which instead of "received gifts among men," paraphrased "gave gifts to men."[1] It must not be supposed that St. Paul quotes the text in *proof* of the Ascension of our Lord—which it would clearly be inadequate and unsuitable to establish : but, speaking of the gifts bestowed by Christ upon the Church, he recalls a passage which, in the form in which he was familiar with it, described a bestowal of gifts on man ; and he cites it as an illustration of what he is saying. St. Paul quotes the Old Testament in the manner common to his age, and not always with that exact regard to the original sense of the passage quoted, which we should expect him to show: he follows, where it suits his purpose, an interpretation current among the Jews, without stopping to inquire whether it was consonant with the sense strictly attaching to the passage in its original connexion. That he does not appeal to the text here as a proof passage, appears further from the fact that there is no indication that the Psalm was treated as a Messianic one, or supposed to have a Messianic sense, by the Jews ; and

[1] This interpretation, at least in the form in which we know it, regarded the verse as referring to *Moses*. The Targum on the Psalms (above, p. 86) renders : " Thou ascendedst up to the firmament, O prophet Moses, thou tookest captives captive, thou didst teach the words of the law, thou gavest them as gifts to the children of men; but the rebellious ones, who become proselytes, turning in penitence, upon them resteth the Shechinah of the glory of Jehovah God." The Syriac Version, the Peshitto, which is also sometimes influenced by Jewish exegesis, has "gave" for "received." The LXX here agrees with the Hebrew.

yet, unless this were antecedently clear, no argument could be based upon it. But St. Paul, in fact, merely quotes the passage, because he sees in it, as understood by the Jews of his own day, an anticipation of a particular truth of Christianity.

The verse, then, in the Psalm is descriptive of a *past* fact ; it describes the historical ascent of God into the "tent" prepared for Him by David upon Zion : it is no prediction of the Ascension of our Lord; it has no reference to the future. At the same time, it is true that, as a signal and conspicuous event in the history of the Old Covenant, it may be viewed as a foreshadowing, or, as it is sometimes termed, a *type*, of the great Ascent and Triumph of Christ, the King, to heaven. And this, no doubt, is the light in which St. Paul really regarded it. The ascent of the Ark, in which God was present, into Zion, *prefigured* the Ascent of Christ into heaven. The captives and spoil, presupposed in the very fact of David's conquest of the stronghold of Zion—though the figure, as used by the Psalmist, must not be interpreted too minutely—and imagined poetically to form part of the procession, *prefigured* the evil powers vanquished by Christ, and, as it were, led visibly in triumph by Him, on the occasion of His return to heaven. Such a view of the work of Christ, as a triumph, is in harmony with St. Paul's thought elsewhere ; for instance, with the passage in which he describes Him as stripping the powers of evil from off Him, and making a show of them openly, triumphing over them upon the Cross.[1] But the gifts received among men cannot, without great artificiality, be taken as prefiguring anything except the *tokens of homage* rendered by men to their ascended Lord. Here St. Paul substitutes a different sense altogether; for material gifts received *from* men, he substitutes spiritual gifts given *to* men. In so doing, however, as has been said, it is probable that he followed a current interpretation, or paraphrase, of the verse, which made it suitable for quotation in a context in which he is speaking of the manifold gifts conferred by Christ upon His Church.

The Psalm breathes the national spirit of ancient Israel. It is a Psalm in which a strain of genuine religious feeling is mingled with notes of battle and victory and vengeance. With Israel's foes in his mind, the Psalmist writes—

> The Lord said, I will bring back from Bashan,
> I will bring them back from the depths of the sea:
> That thou mayest dip thy foot in blood;
> That the tongue of thy dogs may have its portion from the enemy.

So the most evangelical of the prophets does not shrink from describing Israel as a "sharp threshing instrument having teeth," able to beat small and to disperse the powers opposed to it: he does not shrink from threatening Israel's opponents with deadly internecine strife—"And I will feed them that oppress thee with their own flesh; and they shall be

---

[1] Col. ii. 15. Cf. above, p. 189.

drunken with their own blood, as with sweet wine." [1] It could not be otherwise at a time when God's truth was confined within the limits of a particular nation. National and religious interests were inseparably associated ; and the continued existence of the nation, its success against its earthly foes, was the condition on which depended the preservation of the truth committed to it. The long invective against Babylon, which now occupies the greater part of the fiftieth and fifty-first chapters of the Book of Jeremiah,[2] shows how intensely national feeling was aroused, at the prospect of the approaching fall of the great oppressing power. It was just the occasion to call forth such a Psalm as the sixty-eighth,—a triumph-song inspired by the memories of the past, and exultant with the expectation of the future. It was just the occasion also to stir the poet's religious imagination, to suggest to him visions of a future by which the past should be eclipsed. And so he draws his ideal picture of worship in the restored Temple, representing kings as appearing there with offerings, and distant nations as pressing forward to assist. The unnamed poet's triumph-song has become the inheritance of the Christian Church ; and the hopes and aspirations of many hearts, and many times, have found expression in his jubilant, soul-inspiring words. The desire which his opening verses embody is one which we can at all times echo, without the smallest reserve : the majestic ascription

---

[1] Is. xli. 15-16 ; xlix. 26.
[2] Jer. l. 2—li. 58.

of thanksgiving and praise, with which he closes, can never lose its impressiveness, or become inappropriate. The blessings bestowed on Israel, to which the Psalm so abundantly alludes, may be regarded as a figure of the blessings bestowed upon the Church; and hence its suitability as one of the special Psalms for Whitsunday. The triumph of Israel, which it describes or anticipates, may be understood naturally as a figure of the triumph of the Church in its contest with the world, a triumph in part accomplished, in part yet future. Only, in adopting this view of the Psalm, we must be content with the general parallel, we must not, at the risk of indulging in fantastic and arbitrary combinations, seek to accommodate it to minute details. And so, as we recite the Psalm, month by month, and year by year, it may lend words, far nobler than any which we could supply, to the thoughts and feelings appropriate to ourselves; the Psalmist's grateful commemoration of the past, and his joyous anticipations of the future, we may alike transfer to our own lips; his enthusiasm may evoke an echo within our own breasts; our emotions may be stirred, our hearts moved to respond, by the spirit which still swells and throbs in the words of his song.[1]

[1] The writer, in the preceding exposition, has adopted, in doubtful cases, those interpretations which appear to him to be the most probable, though without at all wishing to deny that the Psalm contains passages in which the Hebrew is ambiguous or obscure, and of which a different explanation may conse-

quently be legitimately held. Such variations in detail, however, hardly affect the general sense of the Psalm, as a whole. Even, moreover, should the Psalm, as has been supposed—and there are circumstances not unfavourable to the supposition—be the work of a later age than that to which it has here been referred, the *general* interpretation will still remain the same: it will have been prompted by some occasion *similar* to that which has here been postulated for it: it will remain the expression of the poet's grateful recollections of the past, and of his hopeful anticipations for the future (comp. Cheyne, *Bampton Lectures*, pp. 112 f., 124 f.; *Aids to the Devout Study of Criticism*, 1892, p. 323 ff. ; W. R. Smith, *The Old Testament in the Jewish Church*, ed. 2, pp. 221, 439 f.). Although for historical purposes it is sometimes important to determine, if possible, the date of a Psalm, or other writing, for exegetical purposes it is often sufficient if we are able to re-construct, from the allusions which it contains, the *kind* of occasion out of which it may have sprung, and the situation in which its author may have been placed. Where we can do this, even though it be but approximately, it contributes materially to our comprehension of its contents and scope.

SERMON XI.[1]

THE LORD OUR RIGHTEOUSNESS.

Jer. xxiii. 6: "In his days Judah shall be saved, and Israel shall dwell safely: and this is his name whereby he shall be called, The LORD is our righteousness."

THE Church's year is drawing to a close, and the last of the Sundays after Trinity has from ancient times been celebrated as a kind of eve to Advent. In the lessons appointed for the day, our Church either, as in the First Lesson this morning,[2] views the close of the Christian year as symbolizing the close of human life, or, as in the alternative First Lessons for the afternoon,[3] bids us direct our thoughts towards the coming of Christ. In the Collect we pray God to stir up the wills of His faithful people, and revive them to an energy of service such as we may naturally feel to be needed at a time when we are about

---

[1] Preached in the Cathedral on the last Sunday after Trinity, 1888.

[2] Eccl. xi.-xii.

[3] Hag. ii. 1-9; Mal. iii.-iv. On Hag. ii. 7, see the rendering of the Revised Version; and in illustration of the thought, comp. Is. lx. 5 *end*, 6^b, 7^b, 11^b, 13^b.

to enter upon a new year of Christian life. And in lieu of a passage from an Epistle, our Church, as it does upon exceptional occasions, sets before us a passage from one of the prophets which likewise points our attention to the advent of Christ.

Something is sometimes lost when a passage of Scripture is severed from its original connexion. The first eight verses of the twenty-third chapter of Jeremiah form really the conclusion to the twenty-second chapter, and should be read closely in connexion with it. Jeremiah lived towards the close of the monarchy of Judah, and he passed through experiences more tragic and varied than, so far as we are aware, fell to the lot of any other prophet. His youth was passed in the golden years of Josiah; he lived to see Jerusalem sacked, the Temple burnt, himself an exile in Egypt. But Jeremiah did not merely suffer *with* his nation, at the hand of external foes, he suffered personally at the hand of his fellow-countrymen. Both his denunciations of his people's sins, and the line which he adopted politically,[1] made him unpopular; his life was often in peril; on one occasion the men of his own native place conspired to slay him;[2] on another he was rescued with difficulty from an attempt made in Jerusalem to adjudge him worthy of death;[3] while under Zedekiah the princes of

[1] The policy of submitting to the yoke of the Chaldæans: see (under Jehoiakim, B.C. 604) xxv. 9-12; (under Zedekiah) xxvii. 4-13, and later, during the siege, xxi. 8-10, xxxviii. 2.
[2] Jer. xi. 18-23 (cf. xv. 15, xviii. 18, xx. 7 ff.).
[3] Jer. xxvi.

Judah secured his imprisonment in a loathsome dungeon, from which he was only released through the intercession of a foreigner, who interested himself in his behalf.[1]

In the section of his book which is closed by the passage selected for the Epistle, Jeremiah reviews the lives and characters of three of the last kings of Judah. "Go down to the house of the king of Judah, and speak there this word, and say, Hear the word of the LORD, O king of Judah, that sittest upon the throne of David, thou, and thy servants, and thy people that enter in by these gates. Thus saith the LORD: Execute ye judgment and righteousness, and deliver the spoiled out of the hand of the oppressor: and do no wrong to the stranger, the fatherless, and the widow, neither shed innocent blood in this place. For if ye do this thing indeed, then shall there enter in by the gates of this house kings sitting upon the throne of David, riding in chariots and on horses, he, and his servants, and his people. But if ye will not hear these words, I swear by myself, saith the LORD, that this house shall become a desolation."[2] The judgment on Jehoahaz, who reigned but three months, being at the end of this time deposed by the Egyptians, is a short one: it is confined to the declaration that he shall not return to Jerusalem any more, but "shall die in the place whither they have led him captive, and shall see this land

---

[1] Jer. xxxvii.-xxxviii.   [2] Jer. xxii. 1-5.

no more."[1] It is otherwise with Jehoiakim, whose reign of eleven years was marked by covetousness, and oppression, and judicial murders. Jehoiakim was the vassal of Egypt; he both taxed the people for the purpose of meeting the demands of the Pharaoh,[2] and having a passion for costly buildings, oppressed them further in order to gratify his tastes. " Woe to him that buildeth his house by unrighteousness, and his chambers with injustice; that useth his neighbour's service without wages, and giveth him not his hire; that saith, I will build me a wide house and spacious chambers, and cutteth him out his windows, ceiling it with cedar, and painting it with vermilion.[3] Shalt thou reign, because thou strivest to excel in cedar? did not thy father "—the noble-minded Josiah—" eat and drink, and do judgment and justice? then it was well with him. He judged the cause of the poor and needy; then it was well. Was not this to know me, saith the LORD? But thine eyes and thine heart are set only upon thy dishonest gain, and to shed innocent blood, and upon oppression, and upon violence, for to do it."[4] Josiah, when he died, had been missed and regretted;[5] but Jehoiakim, his son, the prophet adds, shall be "buried with

---

[1] Jer. xxii. 10-12: see 2 Kings xxiii. 33, 34^b.

[2] 2 Kings xxiii. 34^a, 35.

[3] Dividing two words differently, and slightly changing the punctuation, on grammatical grounds, with Hitzig, Payne Smith, Orelli, and others.

[4] Jer. xxii. 13-17.

[5] 2 Kings xxiii. 30^a, 2 Chron. xxxv. 24-25.

the burial of an ass, drawn and cast forth beyond the gates of Jerusalem."

The prophet in tones of pathos begins again : " Go up to Lebanon, and cry; and lift up thy voice in Bashan : and cry from Abarim ; for all thy lovers are destroyed." It is the people of Judah who are addressed, personified as a woman,[1] and bidden thus to lament over the mournful destiny in store for them. " I spake unto thee in thy prosperity ; but thou saidst, I will not hear. This hath been thy manner from thy youth, that thou hast not listened to my voice." And soon he turns to contemplate in particular, with feelings, as it seems, of sympathy and regret, the fate of the third king, Jehoiachin, who after a reign of a hundred days was carried away to Babylon, and languished for thirty years in a Babylonian dungeon. " Is this man Coniah a despised broken vessel? is he a vessel wherein is no pleasure? wherefore are they cast out, he and his seed, and are cast into the land which they know not ? "[2] And then, at

---

[1] The pronouns in the original are feminine. Such personifications are frequent in the prophets : comp., for instance, Jer. vii. 29, x. 17, xlvi. 11. Abarim is named as a height whence the whole land might be viewed (Numb. xxvii. 12). The "lovers" are the nations whose favour Judah had courted (Jer. iv. 30: cf. Ez. xvi. 33, 37), but who will now have to submit to Nebuchadnezzar's yoke, and be powerless to assist her.

[2] xxii. 28. Observe the form of the sentence (a double interrogation, followed by a question introduced by *Wherefore*. . .?) expressive of mingled pathos and surprise, which is peculiar to Jeremiah (ii. 14, 31, viii. 4-5, 19, 22, xiv. 19, xlix. 1, cf. xxx. 6). It is implied that the first two interrogations are to be answered in a negative sense.

THE LORD OUR RIGHTEOUSNESS.

the beginning of the twenty-third chapter, he sums up his verdict upon the kings and rulers of his day in general, under the figure of shepherds who have destroyed and scattered the sheep entrusted to them. The troubles which befel Judah, and led ultimately to its ruin, are traced by Jeremiah to the shortsightedness and studied neglect of those who were its responsible giudes. "Ye have scattered my flock and driven them away, and have not visited them: behold, I will visit upon you the evil of your doings, saith the LORD. And I will gather the remnant of my flock out of all the countries whither I have driven them, and will bring them again to their folds; and they shall be fruitful and multiply. And I will set up shepherds over them, which shall feed them; and they shall fear no more, nor be dismayed, neither shall any be lacking, saith the LORD." The unrighteous rulers will be deposed: wise and just ones,[1] in the happier future which Jeremiah now begins to contemplate, will take their place. There follows the passage from which the text is taken: "Behold, the days come, saith the LORD, that I will raise up unto David a righteous Sprout,[2] and he shall reign as king,

[1] Comp. (for the plural) Jer. iii. 15, Is. i. 26ª, xxxii. 1ᵇ, Mic. v. 5ᵇ.

[2] *Tzemach* is not "a branch" (like *netzer*, Is. xi. 1); it is *shooting foliage* generally. The term is mostly used collectively, as Gen. xix. 25, "the *growth* of the ground," Ps. lxv. 10 (Heb. 11), "Thou blessest the *springing* (*i.e.* the young growth) thereof," Ezek. xvi. 7 (R. V. "bud"), xvii. 9, "the leaves of its *growth*," Is. iv. 2 (see R. V. *marg.*, and Orelli's *Old Testament*

and deal wisely, and shall execute judgment and justice in the land. In his days Judah shall be saved, and Israel shall dwell safely; and this is his name whereby he shall be called, Jehovah is our righteousness." The righteous king whose portrait Jeremiah sketches is the counterpart to the imperfect rulers of his own time. In pointed opposition to Jehoiakim, it is said of him that he will "deal wisely" —deal with such wisdom as shall ensure success[1]— and "execute judgment and justice in the land." Then Israel, no longer the prey of foreign invaders, no longer liable at any moment to be driven into exile, will "dwell safely," under the guardianship of its ideal king.

But in what sense are we to understand the name "Jehovah is our righteousness"? In order to answer this question we must turn to a parallel passage in the prophecies of Jeremiah, where the same expression recurs. Jeremiah is somewhat apt to repeat passages of his prophecies with slight variations of phraseology[2]; and one very similar to this recurs in the great group of prophecies contained in chaps. xxx.—xxxiii., and comprising the comparatively few words of consolation which it was given

---

Prophecy, p. 262), lxi. 10 (R. V. "bud"); but it acquires here an individual sense in virtue of the context. The use in Zech. iii. 8, iv. 12, is based upon this passage.

[1] The force of the word used in the Hebrew. See the margin of the Revised Version: and comp. Josh. i. 7, 1 Sam. xviii. 5, Is. lii. 13 (text and margin likewise).

[2] See the citations in the writer's *Introduction*, p. 259.

him to address to his people. We there read: "In those days, and at that time, will I cause a Sprout of righteousness to grow up unto David; and he shall execute judgment and righteousness in the land. In those days shall Judah be saved, and Jerusalem shall dwell safely: and this is (the name) whereby she shall be called, Jehovah is our righteousness." [1] The name which is applied to the ideal *king* in chap. xxiii. is applied to the ideal *city* in chap. xxxiii.: both alike are to be called by the same significant title, "Jehovah is our righteousness." There is something strange, to our ears, in a name thus formed; but it is in analogy with Hebrew usage. It was the custom of the ancient Israelites to form proper names compounded with one or other of the sacred names more freely than we should do. Thus they gave their children such names as "Jehovah (or God) heareth," or "remembereth," or "judgeth"; [2] or "Jehovah is a help," or "is opulence"; [3] or again, "Jehovah is perfect," or "exalted," or "great." [4] And so we find places named similarly: thus we read of an altar called "Jehovah is my banner," and of another called "Jehovah is peace." [5] Names thus formed were felt, no doubt, to be words of good omen; or they

---

[1] Jer. xxxiii. 15 f.
[2] Shemaiah (or Elishama), Zechariah, Shephatiah, and Jehoshaphat.
[3] Joezer, Joshua (see Job xxxvi. 19, Heb. and R. V.; and cf. xxxiv. 19).
[4] Jotham, Jehoram, Gedaliah.
[5] Ex. xvii. 15; Jud. vi. 24.

were intended to mark what either was, or was hoped to be a reality. The prophets, by an extension of this usage, not unfrequently employ the *name* as the mark of a character, to be given to a person or place because the idea which it expressed was really inherent in him or it. Thus Isaiah, speaking of the ideal Zion of the future, says: "Afterward thou shalt be called The city of righteousness, the faithful city"[1] —called so, namely, because the qualities of righteousness and faithfulness, so sadly lacking in the existing city, will be conspicuous in it. And Ezekiel, speaking of the restored Zion, says, in the last verse of his book: "And the name of the city from that day shall be, Jehovah is there"; he imagines, that is, a symbolical title, summing up in a brief and forcible manner the characteristic state or condition of the city.[2]

The case is similar in Jeremiah. The city bears a name indicating the character of its inhabitants: God is the source and ground of their righteousness. Jerusalem is to become the home and abode of righteousness, through the gracious operation of her God. Here a similar name is given to the ideal king, or Messiah. He is the pledge and symbol to Israel that their righteousness was to have its source in God. Just as Isaiah, when Judah was sorely tried by external foes, had given his ideal king the symbolical name of *God is with us*,[3] as a guarantee that

[1] Is. i. 26.
[2] Ez. xlviii. 35. For other examples of the same usage see Is. iv. 3, xxx. 7, lxii. 2, 4, 12, Jer. xx. 3, Hos. i. 10^b, etc.
[3] Is. vii. 14^b (see R. V. *marg.*); comp. viii. 8^b, 10^b.

THE LORD OUR RIGHTEOUSNESS. 213

the Divine help would be assured to them; so Jeremiah, at a time when the character of the people had largely deteriorated, gives him the symbolical name of *Jehovah is our righteousness*, significant of the fact that the nation's righteousness can only be assured by God.[1] The ideal ruler whom Jeremiah foresees will govern his nation with wisdom and success; and under his gracious administration, the divinely imparted character of righteousness will be realized by the nation.

Jeremiah does not state in the passage *how* he conceives this state of righteousness to be brought about; he does not even connect it distinctly with the work of the ideal ruler. Jeremiah pictures the Messiah as the author of *civic* righteousness;[2] but the question how far this pre-supposes righteousness in the heart of the *individual*, or how far the latter is to be conceived as involved in the Messiah's work, does not seem to have been present to his mind. To a certain extent the passage may be supplemented by another, in which, speaking of the New Covenant

---

[1] The analogy of other compound proper names shows that this is the correct rendering of the name (so R. V.), not that of A. V., "The LORD our righteousness," as Orelli (*l. c.* p. 334 f.) rightly observes. The significance of the name lies not in the fact that the Messiah would be termed "Jehovah our righteousness," but in its expressing, like Immanuel ("God *is* with us," not "God with us"), the relation of God to His Church. Similarly Keil, in his Commentary, *ad loc.*

[2] "Shall do judgment and justice in the land": the same phrase is used of David, 2 Sam. viii. 15; of Solomon, 1 Kings x. 9; of Josiah, Jer. xxii. 15.

to be concluded in the future with the people, he says: "After those days, saith the LORD, I will put my law in their inward parts, and write it in their hearts ; and I will be their God, and they shall be my people. And they shall teach no more every man his neighbour, and every man his brother, saying, Know the LORD : for they shall all know me, from the least of them unto the greatest of them, saith the LORD : for I will forgive their iniquity, and their sin will I remember no more."[1] Here Jeremiah promises the advent of an ideal state, in which the sin of the people is forgiven, and its nature transformed; in which Israel shall be no longer subject to law as a command imposed from without, but shall be ruled by impulses to good, acting upon the heart as a principle operative from within. In other words, Jeremiah anticipates what St. Paul terms a "new creature,"—the re-creation by a Divine act of man's inner nature. But in neither passage does Jeremiah explain how, or by what mediate agency, he conceived human nature to be thus turned to righteousness—the more complete delineation of the picture was reserved for the future. Nevertheless, as has been said,[2] these two passages of the prophet contain *in nuce* the fundamental doctrines of the Gospel. The New Covenant is to be a state of righteousness in the Church, effected by a Divine act of grace, having its source in God, constituted and guaranteed by Him. "Jehovah *is* our righteousness," says the prophet,

[1] Jer. xxxi. 33-34.   [2] Orelli, *l. c.* p. 335 f.

using a pregnant Hebrew idiom, expressing that He is the ground and source and guarantee of our righteousness—just as we read in Ps. lxviii., for instance, that "God *is* our salvation";[1] but the relation in which Jeremiah conceived his righteous king to stand towards the individual Israelite is not distinctly expressed; and hence we are left in uncertainty whether he so far anticipated the teaching of the New Testament as to view this righteousness as conferred through the agency of the same ideal ruler, whose name is designed as the symbol of the fact. The terms in which he speaks, however, do not suggest that he conceived him as the author of justification, in the theological sense of the term; they imply rather that he pictured him as ensuring, by his wise and just administration, the *conditions* under which righteousness of life might be maintained effectually among the people.

This, then, is the aspect under which we may view the prophecy of Jeremiah. Interpreting his words in the light of the future, and translating them into Christian phraseology, we may say that they teach us to look to God, as the source of our righteousness through Christ, and to the Church as the sphere in which, by the means which He has appointed, this righteousness may be obtained. And so the lesson comes suitably as an introduction to the season of Advent. It suggests to us one of the most funda-

[1] Ps. lxviii. 19 (Heb. 20). See the Revised Version. The rendering of the Authorized Version is inexact.

mental principles of our Christian faith. It points us to the ideal of human life, to the ground on which it rests, to the Advent of Christ, as providing the means for effectually realizing it. It bids us contemplate Him as the just and perfect ruler of men, and as the ever-present embodiment of the truth that "The LORD is our righteousness." True, the ideal state foreshadowed by Jeremiah has not yet been realized: the law of God is not yet written so indelibly upon the hearts of men, that all can be said to act upon it instinctively, or that we can yet afford, as some strange sectaries have imagined that we could afford, to dispense with teachers and instructors, and other methods of reminding us what that law is. But it is upon a profound sense of the requirements of human nature that the prophet's declaration is based; and it is one of the most far-reaching and comprehensive anticipations of the ultimate destiny of human history which are to be found in the Old Testament Scriptures. It sets vividly before us what should be the aim of our endeavours, and the goal of our aspiration. And so, every time that, in our public services, the Decalogue is recited, it is followed by the petition, expressed in the very words of the prophet, that the laws of which it is the sum may be "written in our hearts." May God's laws, as we thus pray, be written in our hearts; and may we realize effectively for ourselves the truth that "The LORD is our righteousness"!

SERMON XII.[1]

MERCY, AND NOT SACRIFICE.

Hos. vi. 6: " For I desire mercy, and not sacrifice, and the knowledge of God more than burnt offerings."

SUCH are the words — familiar to us from their quotation on two occasions by our Blessed Lord — with which the prophet Hosea recalls his contemporaries to a true sense of what God demands from His worshippers. Hosea prophesied in the Northern Kingdom, and the greater part of his prophetical book[2] dates from the troubled and anxious years, about the middle of the eighth century, B.C., through which the kingdom of Ephraim was hastening to its doom.[3] The dynasty founded by Jehu had reached its term: party spirit, which there was now no strong hand to curb, reigned unchecked; short-lived kings arose, who were able to retain their position for only a few months or years; rival factions, at issue with

---

[1] Preached in the Cathedral, on the 10th Sunday after Trinity, 1889.

[2] Viz. chaps. iv.-xiv.

[3] Chaps. iv.-xiv. were probably written during the reign of Menahem (see 2 Kings xv. 17-22, cf. 14-16), B.C. 745-737. Samaria was captured by Sargon, King of Assyria, B.C. 722.

each other, invoked alternately the aid of Egypt and
Assyria, hoping thereby to secure themselves, if not
to save the State at the same time, from ruin.[1] Their
efforts were of no avail. Hoshea, the last king, who
owed his throne to the assistance of the Assyrians,[2]
broke with them, and opened treasonable negotiations
with Egypt; the result was that the Assyrians laid
siege to Samaria, and after three years took it, transporting many of its inhabitants to different parts
of the Assyrian empire, and bringing thereby the
history of the Northern Kingdom to its close.

Hosea, however, prophesied before the catastrophe
actually arrived, though he saw with sufficient distinctness the disaster that was imminent.[3] He saw
that the political and social disorder in Ephraim had
advanced too far to be retrieved; and his pages, few
though they are, present a vivid picture of the self-indulgence of the leaders of the nation, resulting in
the degradation of public life, and decay of the
nation's strength.[4] The consequences of Israel's evil
conduct and policy are summed up by him in the
epigrammatic phrase, which speaks with terrible
suggestiveness: "For they sow the wind, and they
shall reap the whirlwind," adding, with a change of

---

[1] Comp. Hos. v. 13, vii. 11, viii. 9, xii. 1.

[2] "Pekah, their king, I slew: Hoshea (to rule) over them
I appointed," says Tiglath-Pileser in an inscription of B.C. 734
(Schrader, *Cuneiform Inscriptions and the Old Testament*, p.
255 f.). This fact is not mentioned in the narrative of Kings.

[3] *E.g.* Hos. v. 14, vii. 16, viii. 14, ix. 6, 11-17, x. 14-15.

[4] *E.g.* Hos. vii. 3-7.

figure, as if to cut off even the last desperate chance of escape: "It hath no stalk: the blade shall yield no meal; if so be it yield, strangers shall swallow it up."[1] Nor is Israel morally what it should be: the picture that he draws is darker than would have been thought possible. "Hear the word of the LORD, ye children of Israel: for the LORD hath a controversy with the inhabitants of the land: there is no faithfulness,[2] nor kindness, nor knowledge of God in the land. There is nought but swearing and breaking faith, and killing, and stealing, and committing adultery: they break through (every bond), and blood toucheth blood"[3]—forming, as it were, a continuous stream. The priests, whose duty it was to teach the people the moral precepts of God, were not the least offenders: they "feed on the sin of my people, and set their heart on their iniquity," *i. e.* instead of striving to check iniquity, they long to see it abound, in order that their own perquisites, derived from the people's offerings, may be the greater.[4] They even went further than this: they outraged the law openly: they formed bands for the purpose of intercepting and murdering pilgrims journeying to the sanctuaries.[5] The king and princes are represented as taking a delight in schemes of lawlessness and wrong.[6] Thus

[1] Hos. viii. 7.
[2] *I. e.* honesty, integrity: in his dealings with his neighbour no one can be depended upon. The meaning of the term will be apparent from 2 Kings xii. 15 [Heb. 16], xxii. 7.
[3] Hos. iv. 1-2: cf. vi. 7-10, vii. 1-2.   [4] Hos. iv. 6-9, esp. 8.
[5] Hos. vi. 9.   [6] Hos. vii. 3.

anarchy and civil war, combined with an unspiritual religion and lax morality, are bringing Northern Israel to the verge of ruin. And Ephraim, though adversity or disappointment may impel him to call upon Jehovah with his lips, or seek to propitiate Him with his sacrifices,[1] shows no sign of genuine repentance.

Hence the prophet, speaking in Jehovah's name, exclaims: "O Ephraim, what shall I do unto thee? O Judah, what shall I do unto thee? for your goodness is as a morning cloud, and as the dew that goeth early away."[2] The "goodness"—*i. e.* dutiful affection and love, whether towards God or man—which Israel affects, is superficial and evanescent. "Therefore have I hewed them by the prophets; I have slain them by the words of my mouth: and my judgment goeth forth as the light."[3] Israel's persistent disregard of Jehovah's fundamental demands has provoked His interference: He has warned them, in unsparing words, of the fatal issue of their conduct; and now His judgment is prepared to issue forth, as conspicuous to all as the light of the rising dawn. "For I desire mercy, and not sacrifice, and knowledge of God more than burnt offerings." The word rendered *mercy* in this verse is the same as that rendered *goodness* in verse 4,—a fact made evident in the Revised Version by the same marginal alternative," Or, *kindness*," attached to both. "Mercy" is in fact too narrow a rendering: mercy—as Portia's famous speech in the

---

[1] Comp. Hos. ii. 7ᵇ, v. 6, vii. 14, viii. 2.
[2] Hos. vi. 4.   [3] Hos. vi. 5 (R. V. *marg.*).

MERCY, AND NOT SACRIFICE. 221

Merchant of Venice may remind us—is the quality by which a person abstains, out of motives of benevolence or compassion, from exercising his legitimate rights against one who stands towards him at a disadvantage—as when a person, for instance, who has been injured, renounces his right to exact vengeance or punishment of the offender: but the quality here intended by Hosea is wider than this; it is a quality exercised mutually amongst equals; it is the regard and consideration in intercourse with one another, which, when observed in society generally, makes life tolerable, and forms the bond by which the whole community is knit together.[1] It is that kindliness of feeling, which Hosea had previously deplored as lacking among the Israelites, and the absence of which was accompanied by such a flagrant disregard of their duty towards their neighbour.[2] It is the same virtue which Hosea demands elsewhere:[3] "And thou, turn thou to thy God: keep mercy and judgment, and wait on thy God continually,"—turn unto God, and prove the reality of thy penitence by dealing towards men with blended kindness and justice, and cherishing towards God a spirit of trustful

---

[1] The sense of חֶסֶד appears perhaps most plainly from its use in the common phrase, "to do *chésed* and faithfulness with a person," Gen. xxiv. 49 (R. V., "deal kindly and truly with"). xlvii. 29; Josh. ii. 14; 2 Sam. ii. 6. (R. V., "shew kindness and truth to") *i.e.* to show towards one the kindness and faithfulness of a true friend (comp. Ex. xxxiv. 6, of Jehovah, "plenteous in kindness and faithfulness"; also "kindness" alone, Gen. xxiv. 12, 14, xl. 14; 2 Sam. ii. 5, ix. 1, 3, 7, &c.).
[2] Hos. iv. 1ᵇ. [3] Hos. xii. 6.

faith. It is an aspect of that quality of *love*, which, as the bond uniting God and His people, as well as the individual Israelites to each other, is a fundamental element in Hosea's teaching. Hosea conceives the relation of Jehovah to His people as a *moral union*, marked by affection and regard on the one side, and demanding a corresponding affection and regard on the other. In the first three chapters of his prophecy, the figure of the marriage-tie is beautifully and touchingly applied for the purpose of symbolizing this: we have set before us successively the choice and affection of the husband, the reciprocal fidelity and loyalty and love, which for a while ensued, then the faithlessness and the breach [1]; after this, finally, not the husband's permanent alienation, but, after the necessary discipline, His willingness, if she shows herself to be sincerely penitent, to renew His past relations with His erring spouse, and even to make the bond between them closer and dearer than it had been before.[2] Elsewhere, another type of domestic affection supplies the figure under which the same prophet exemplifies the patient and loving regard which had from the first been displayed by Jehovah towards His people. "When Israel was a child, then I loved him, and called my son out of Egypt." But Israel's response was imperfect: "The more they"—*i.e.* God's messengers—" called them, the more they went from them: they sacrificed unto the Baals,[3] and burnt

---

[1] Hos. ii. 2-13.   [2] Hos. ii. 14-23, esp. 19-20.
[3] *I.e.* the various local, or special, Baals, worshipped at differ-

incense to graven images. And yet I had taught Ephraim to go, taking them on my arms[1]; but they knew not that I healed them "; they were unconscious of the providence watching over their welfare, and assisting in the development of their national strength. "I drew them with cords of a man, with bands of love; and I was to them as they that take off the yoke on their jaws, and I laid meat unto them."[2] Not with violence, but gently, with tender indulgence and consideration, had they been treated; Jehovah had shown towards them the love and regard of a father. But Israel, as an ideal community, is Jehovah's spouse; and Israel, as an aggregate of individual persons, is Jehovah's family; and between the members of a family governed by such a Head, mutual loyalty and kindness, mutual consideration and regard, ought instinctively to prevail, and form a natural bond regulating the intercourse of each with his fellow-man.[3]

---

ent places, or under particular titles. On Phœnician inscriptions we read, for instance, of Baal of Tyre, Baal of Lebanon, Baal of Tarsus, Baal of Heaven, Baal Hammān (*i.e.*, the Solar Baal), &c. Comp. the writer's *Notes on the Hebrew Text of Samuel* (1890), p. 50 f.

[1] Slightly emending the existing Hebrew text (אֶקָּחֵם עַל זְרוֹעֹתָי).

[2] Hos. xi. 1-4; comp. iii. 1, and (in the promise for the future) xiv. 4. *Cords of a man*, i. e. "not with the violence suited to an unruly heifer (cf. x. 11), but with the 'cords of men' (*i. e.* such as men can bear), did Jehovah win His people's obedience" (Cheyne, *ad loc.*).

[3] On the characteristic teaching of Hosea, see more fully the excellent chapter on Hosea in W. R. Smith's *Prophets of Israel*, p. 154 ff.; or the Introduction to Prof. Cheyne's useful

"For I desire kindness, and not sacrifice, and the knowledge of God more than burnt offerings." By "knowledge of God," Hosea here means not a merely intellectual apprehension of His nature, but a knowledge displaying itself in conduct, a knowledge of His power, His influence, and His character, resting upon spiritual experience, and resulting in moral practice. A passage of Jeremiah explains the sense in which the expression is to be understood. Speaking of the just and virtuous Josiah, and contrasting him with his degenerate son Jehoiakim, Jeremiah says: "He judged the cause of the poor and the needy, then it was well (with him). *Was not this to know me?* saith the Lord. But thine eyes and thine heart are set only upon thy dishonest gain, and to shed innocent blood, and upon oppression, and upon violence, for to do it." The "knowledge" of God is identified here with equity, justice, unselfishness, philanthropy—in a word, with the due observance of those moral duties which the society in which we live, and our relation to other men, impose upon us—the very opposite of the violence, and oppression, and self-assertion of which Jehoiakim was guilty, and

---

and sympathetic Commentary on this prophet in the *Cambridge Bible for Schools and Colleges*, pp. 15 ff., 22 ff. The truth that Jehovah *loves* Israel (Hos. iii. 1, ix. 15, xi. 1, 4, xiv. 4), if the date assigned by critics to Deuteronomy be right (for it is found in that book, Deut. vii. 8, 13, x. 15, xxiii. 5), is a new idea in the religious conceptions of Israel. In subsequent prophets the idea recurs—Jer. xxxi. 3; Is. xliii. 4; lxiii. 9; Mal. i. 2; and of the future, Zeph. iii. 17.

which were rife in Hosea's day in the kingdom of Israel. The Israelites, Hosea says, had misapprehended the nature of Jehovah's demands: they were prompt, and even punctilious, in the performance of outward religious ceremonies, supposing that this would satisfy His requirements; but what He delighted in was conduct governed consistently by a moral purpose, and a life regulated by a cheerful regard for the rights and needs of other men: sacrifice was offered properly as the *expression* of a right state of heart, but it could not be accepted in lieu of it; it was valueless unless accompanied by sincerity of purpose and integrity of life.

Mankind have in all ages shown a readiness to conform with the external forms and offices of religion, while heedless of its spiritual precepts, and of the claim which it makes to regulate their conduct and their life. The faults that have been thus indulged in under the cloke of religion have differed: sometimes they have been worldliness, ambition, sensual indulgence; sometimes they have been injustice, oppression, hard-heartedness, and the many other modes in which a love of dishonest gain manifests itself; sometimes they have consisted in spiritual pride, vanity, and exclusiveness; and it has been the aim of every great religious reform, and of every great spiritual teacher, to awaken in men a sense of what the profession of a religion really involves, and to bring them to understand the virtue of consistency.

Thus the teaching of Hosea is not different from that of the other great prophets on the same subject. Amos, writing a few years earlier, represents God as repudiating indignantly the offerings and services of the Israelites: "I hate, I reject your pilgrimages, and I will take no delight in your solemn assemblies... Take thou away from me the noise of thy songs: for I will not hear the melody of thy viols. But let judgment roll down as waters, and righteousness as an ever-flowing stream."[1] And Isaiah, a few years later, speaks in the same strain, alluding contemptuously to the formal observance of religious services, or, as we should say, of Church-going, as *Temple-treading*[2]: "To what purpose is the multitude of your sacrifices unto me? saith the LORD: I am full of the burnt offerings of rams, and the fat of fed beasts; and I delight not in the blood of bullocks, or of lambs, or of he-goats. When ye come to appear before me, who hath required this at your hand, to *trample my courts?* ... Your new moons and your appointed feasts my soul hateth: they are a cumbrance unto me; I am weary to bear them... Wash you, make you clean; put away the evil of your doings from before my eyes; cease to do evil: learn to do well; seek judgment, set right the oppressor, judge the fatherless, plead for the widow."[3]

[1] Amos v. 21, 23, 24.
[2] G. A. Smith, *The Book of Isaiah* in the "Expositor's Bible," vol. i. (1888), p. 7.
[3] Is. i. 11, 12, 14, 16, 17.

And another prophet, writing probably in the dark days of Manasseh, having represented the people as asking: "Wherewith shall I come before Jehovah, and bow myself before the high God? shall I come before him with burnt offerings, with calves a year old? Will Jehovah be pleased with thousands of rams, or with ten thousands of rivers of oil? shall I give my firstborn for my transgression, the fruit of my body for the sin of my soul?" meets their question with the humiliating reply: "He hath shewed thee, O man, what is good; and what doth Jehovah require of thee, but to do justly, and to love *kindness*, and to walk humbly with thy God?"[1]

In the days of Christ, the temper manifested by the Israelites of an earlier age had become intensified, and the practices which were the expression of it had been reduced to system. The spirit of legalism had become all-powerful; and those who were not absorbed in worldly interests, and indifferent to religion altogether, were spell-bound under its influence. The aim of the teachers of the day, in their own language, was to set a "fence" about the law[2]—to guard the letter of the law against violation by surrounding it

[1] Mic. vi. 6-8. Comp. also Jer. vi. 20, vii. 1-15.
[2] "Make a fence about the law," is one of the maxims, quoted from the teachers of a former generation, with which the treatise of the Mishnah called *Pirkê Abhoth* opens. See C. Taylor's edition, published under the title *Sayings of the Jewish Fathers* (1877), p. 26; also Ewald, *History of Israel*, v. p. 195; Kuenen, *Religion of Israel*, iii. pp. 2, 15; Edersheim, *Life and Times of Jesus*, i. pp. 95, 98, 100 f.

with by-rules, which increased in minuteness and complexity until they threatened to cover the whole field of human conduct. This multiplication of rules naturally gave rise, firstly, to contrivances for evading them when they became intolerably burdensome; and secondly, to the neglect of the very system which they were intended to guard, by the attention being unduly concentrated upon outward conformity with the rule. The consequence was that a ceremonialism arose far in excess of that combated by Hosea or Isaiah, from which followed inevitably the spiritual vices of ostentation, vanity, and self-complacency, on the part of those who were obedient to the letter of the law, combined with censoriousness towards any of their neighbours who evinced a disregard for such observances. These are the faults of the Pharisees, as they stand before us in the pages of the Gospels. The importance attached to the newly-devised rules, the so-called "fence" about the law, forming a burden to the shoulders, heavy to be borne[1]; the sophistical evasions, as, for instance, that by which a man escaped the duty of providing for his parents[2]; the scrupulousness with which the tithe on mint, and anise, and cummin was paid, while justice, mercy, and faith were unheeded; the cup and the platter clean without, but within full of extortion and excess; the prayers said at street corners, and alms proclaimed with the trumpet; the thanks rendered for being an exemplar of virtue and piety, and the contempt of

[1] Matthew xxiii. 4.   [2] Matthew xv. 5; Mark vii. 11.

publicans, and all base wicked people [1]—these are the habits and principles which characterize the Pharisees, in whom the religion of the Old Testament became finally de-spiritualized, and the hollowness and unreality of whose pretensions were exposed in the denunciations uttered against them by Christ. It is natural that, in doing this, our Lord should revert to the purer spiritual perceptions possessed by the older prophets, and point His hearers to writings, the authority of which they would recognize themselves. The verse from Hosea is quoted by Him twice.[2] Once when the Pharisees complained that He took meals with publicans and sinners, and He replied: "They that are whole have no need of a physician but they that are sick. But go ye and learn what this meaneth, 'I desire mercy, and not sacrifice': for I came not to call the righteous, but sinners." The attitude of mind which shrank from consorting with the "publicans," or tax-gatherers, whom the Pharisees abhorred, and the "sinners," whom they viewed with lofty disdain, is here shown by Christ to be incompatible with the spirit of charity and affectionate regard towards our fellow-creatures, inculcated by the prophet of old. The other occasion was when His disciples began to pluck and eat the ears of corn on the Sabbath. The legalists of Christ's day regarded desecration of the Sabbath, even in the minutest particular, as a most heinous offence, and

---

[1] Matthew xxiii. 23, 25 ; vi. 2, 5; Luke xviii. 11 f.
[2] Matthew ix. 13 ; xii. 7.

extraordinary provisions were framed by them with the object of securing its due observance. To pluck, and, as St. Luke adds,[1] to rub ears of corn in the hand, were, respectively, species of reaping and threshing; they were accordingly declared unlawful[2]; and being indulged in by the disciples, they at once elicited from the Pharisees the unfriendly comment: "Behold thy disciples do that which it is not lawful to do upon the Sabbath day." Our Lord, after referring His objectors to the example of David, and the regular practice of the priests, adds: "But if ye had known what this meaneth, 'I desire mercy, and not sacrifice,' ye would not have condemned the guiltless." That is, their condemnation of the disciples proceeded from a perverted sentiment. Ceremonial observances constituted in their eyes the whole of religion: hence they passed a harsh, inconsiderate judgment on the manner in which on the Sabbath day the disciples had satisfied the cravings of hunger: they had not learnt the lesson which their own prophet taught, and had condemned in consequence men who were innocent.

Mercy, and not sacrifice! The knowledge of God, rather than burnt offerings! The saying is one of those pregnant ones which abound in the writings of the prophets, and which, expanded and generalized, became the basis of the teaching of Christ. Christ emancipated His contemporaries, and through them

[1] Luke vi. 1.
[2] Comp. Edersheim, *Life and Times of Jesus*, ii. pp. 56, 780.

the generations to come, from the bondage of the letter; and though the lesson which He taught has sometimes been obscured, sometimes been on the point of fading from the memory of His Church, He has left an example and a method which could not be mistaken, and to which reformers in successive ages might turn as to a beacon in the gloom. Christ enforced anew, more comprehensively than could be done by the prophets who lived while the older Dispensation was still in force, and who had no thought of overthrowing it, the true character of religion, the true righteousness of the Kingdom of Heaven. True religion had its seat in the heart; it did not consist in conformity with rules. Religious observances had their value for the purpose of preserving the spiritual life, for giving expression to feelings of gratitude or devotion, for addressing petitions to the Most High, or as being the appointed channels for the reception of Divine grace: it was an abuse to take those institutions, which were most completely of a formal and ceremonial character to make them an end in themselves, and to treat their observance as constituting the whole duty of man. Of one of the most sacred institutions of the older Dispensation Christ did not shrink from saying: "The Sabbath was made for man, and not man for the Sabbath." The citizen of the Kingdom of Heaven was recognized, not by external marks, but by Godlike dispositions, by humility, meekness, the aspiration after goodness, simplicity. The law of charity, of forgiveness, of philanthropy, of mercy, took the place

of the law of works and ceremonial observances.
And thus Christ was enabled also to teach a new
doctrine as to man. Those whom the Jews at large
viewed as aliens—though here too He had the prophets
as His predecessors [1]—He invited into His fold :
those whom the Pharisees treated as outcasts, He
befriended. He taught the worth of the individual
man, irrespectively of possessions, position, or character; and He did this practically by loving the
neglected, the people of no social account. He
taught, further, a larger conception of God, a conception of God not only as the Father of the Hebrew
nation,[2] or its royal Head, but as the Father of the
individual and of the race, as One who bestows His
gifts of nature equally upon all, who is ready to enter
with all into relations of grace, and who turns the
eye of His favour rather towards the penitent publican
than towards the self-satisfied and exclusive religionist.
And thus the moral teachings of the prophets, broadened, deepened, enlarged, merge in Christ's doctrine
of the true righteousness of the Kingdom of Heaven.

[1] *E.g.* Is. ii. 2-3, xix. 23-5; Jer. iii. 17; Zeph. iii. 9; Is. xlii. 1ᵇ, 4,ᵇ xlix. 6ᵇ, li. 4ᵇ, lvi. 6-7, &c.
[2] Is. lxiii. 16, lxiv. 8 (above, p. 190); comp. Deut. xxxii. 6; Jer. iii. 19, xxxi. 9; Mal. ii. 10; also Ps. lxviii. 5, ciii. 13.

THE END.

www.ingramcontent.com/pod-product-compliance
Lightning Source LLC
Chambersburg PA
CBHW070246230426
43664CB00014B/2420